With set works for examinations from summer 2013 onwards

D.

A2 Music
Study Guide

AQA

Richard Knight

Music Study Guides

GCSE, AS and A2 Music Study Guides (AQA, Edexcel and OCR)
GCSE, AS and A2 Music Listening Tests (AQA, Edexcel and OCR)
GCSE, AS and A2 Music Revision Guides (AQA, Edexcel and OCR)
AS/A2 Music Technology Study Guide (Edexcel)
AS/A2 Music Technology Listening Tests (Edexcel)
AS/A2 Music Technology Revision Guides (Edexcel)

Also available from Rhinegold Education

Key Stage 3 Listening Tests: Book 1 and Book 2
AS and A2 Music Harmony Workbooks
GCSE and AS Music Composition Workbooks
GCSE and AS Music Literacy Workbooks
Dictionary of Music in Sound
Understanding Popular Music
Music Technology from Scratch
Musicals in Focus, Baroque Music in Focus, Film Music in Focus

First published 2012 in Great Britain by
Rhinegold Education
14–15 Berners Street
London W1T 3LJ, UK
www.rhinegoldeducation.co.uk

© 2012 Rhinegold Education
a division of Music Sales Limited

You should always check the current requirements of the examination, since these may change.
Copies of the AQA Specification can be downloaded from the AQA website at www.aqa.org.uk or may be
purchased from AQA publications, Unit Two, Wheel Forge Way, Trafford Park, Manchester M17 1EH.
Telephone: 0844 209 6614 Fax: 0161 953 1177 Email: publications@aqa.org.uk

AQA A2 Music Study Guide 4th edition
Order No. RHG102
ISBN: 978-1-78038-492-4

Exclusive Distributors:
Music Sales Ltd
Distribution Centre, Newmarket Road, Bury St Edmunds,
Suffolk IP33 3YB, UK

Printed in the EU

Contents

The author

Richard Knight read music at St John's College, Oxford, and has been director of music at two leading independent schools. He now combines teaching with work as a principal examiner at A level and is on the panel of examiners for the ABRSM. Richard has written a number of study guides and revision guides for Rhinegold Education, and is a frequent contributor to *Music Teacher* magazine.

As a composer, Richard has a large catalogue of works to his name, covering orchestral, chamber, church and school music. Recent works have included a setting of Hail to the Lord's Anointed for a school choir tour to New York, a set of four pieces for tango quintet, and a serenade for oboe and two clarinets. His first opera, *All to Play For*, is due to be produced in April 2013. Richard has a particular interest in all things South American.

Acknowledgements

The author would like to thank the consultant Paul Terry, and the editorial and design team of Elizabeth Boulton, Harriet Power and Christina Forde for their expert support in the preparation of this book.

Introduction

About the course

The AQA specification for A2 Music follows a very similar structure to the AS course you will already have completed, and much will seem familiar. From September 2009 the course consists of three units:

➢ Unit 4 – Written Examination: Music in Context: 40%

➢ Unit 5 – Composing: Developing Musical Ideas: 30%

➢ Unit 6 – Performing: A Musical Performance: 30%.

This specification follows on from the AS qualification administered by AQA. If you have changed centre between AS and A2 and your AS Music is awarded by one of the other boards, you will need to point this out to the Examinations Officer at your new centre immediately, so that special arrangements can be made for you.

Unit 4

For this paper you are required to:

➢ Listen to some unprepared excerpts of music, and answer questions that will test your aural perception and ability to understand some of the details of the music you hear

➢ Study one from a choice of two set works taken from the compulsory Area of Study, 'The Western Classical Tradition', and answer questions on two selected passages of the work and write one longer essay

➢ Write an essay on another Historical Area of Study new for A2 level.

There should be regular time given to studying the set work and the material needed for the second Area of Study during the year. You will also need to have regular practice to further train your aural skills for Section A of the paper. Your exam answers will be sent to an AQA examiner for marking.

Unit 5

Composing is done as coursework over a timed period of 20 hours, during which you have to complete **one** of the following briefs:

➢ Two exercises in compositional techniques

➢ A 5- to 8-minute composition

➢ An arrangement of a set piece of 'classical' music into a pop, rock, or jazz idiom.

Whichever brief you choose to tackle, you must also complete a Review to evaluate the success of your work.

The specific briefs will be available for you from 1 November. There should be plenty of opportunity to develop your compositional skills before and after that date. Your completed coursework will be sent to an AQA examiner for marking by 15 May.

Unit 6

For this unit you have to submit recordings of a short programme of performances lasting between 10 and 15 minutes. This must comprise at least two contrasting pieces. The performances may be:

➢ Solo acoustic performances

➢ Technology-based performances

> A mix of solo acoustic and technology-based performances in which each category comprises at least 5 minutes of the overall programme.

Recordings for this unit need to be completed and sent to an AQA examiner for marking by 15 May.

About this guide

The work for A2 Music builds on what you will already have covered in your AS Music course. Indeed the course is structured in a very similar way: you will be tested in aural perception, knowledge of a set work, awareness of an historical study, compositional skill (whether techniques, free composition or arranging), and performing ability (acoustic or technology-based). In A2 each of these areas will be pursued to a more advanced degree.

This book will help you prepare for the exam by providing further material to advance your listening skills for Section A of Unit 4, as well as detailed analyses of the two set works for Section B (Elgar and Shostakovich), and information on some representative works for whichever area of study you choose for Section C. There is also guidance for developing your skills in the techniques required for completing the Unit 5 briefs, and advice on how to prepare for the Unit 6 performances.

Like the AS examination, the A2 course is usually covered in less than a single year: you normally start in September and the coursework is due in mid-May with the Unit 4 examination in June. Given this time pressure, there are various activities which you can undertake by yourself to improve your chances of success at this level:

> Regular listening to music – remember *listening* requires active involvement in the aural experience, thinking about what is being played; it is not the same as the passive process of *hearing* music.

> Becoming familiar with your set work – you should try to listen through your set work frequently and regularly; best of all, look for an opportunity to hear it live in the concert hall.

> Expanding your knowledge of your chosen historical study through exploring the repertoire with both recorded and live performances, perhaps playing some of the music yourself, and reading about the background to the topic.

> Developing your compositional skills by inventing and experimenting with musical ideas frequently, using both your imagination and your powers of analysis.

> Sustained practice for your performance, either through systematic instrumental work in readiness for the acoustic performance, or frequent work with the software you will be using for the technology-based performances.

Help for all these activities can be found in this book. You will also be able to make the most of the work your teacher covers with you if you use this study guide to prepare for your lessons, especially on your set work.

All of this will help to develop your understanding of the music you will be meeting during the A2 course and the musical skills that are required for success at this level. It should also make your course stimulating, fulfilling and enjoyable. The best of luck!

Unit 4:
Music in Context

For this unit you will have to take a written paper which lasts for 2 hours 15 minutes. It accounts for 40% of the A2 examination (or 20% of your overall A level). There will be three sections:

➤ Section A   Listening (40 marks, approximately 45 minutes)

➤ Section B   Historical Study: Area of Study 1 – The Western Classical Tradition (40 marks)

➤ Section C   Historical Study: Area of Study 3 (20 marks).

Section A requires listening to a recording of musical extracts on which questions are set. You will be familiar with this kind of examination from GCSE and AS Music. Once the recording has finished, the remainder of the exam will be conducted under normal exam conditions, so you will be able to check your answers to Section A and tackle the essay questions for Sections B and C.

You are allowed to take into the exam room a 'clean' copy of your chosen set work – i.e. one without any analytical markings – to help you in Section B. You are not allowed to take with you scores for Section C.

Note that at A2 this written unit has a heavier weighting than the equivalent (Unit 1) at AS.

Section B is seen as the continuation of Area of Study 1 in the AS course; Section C is called 'Area of Study 3', since the AS specification included 'Area of Study 2'.

Section A: Listening

Revision of AS Listening

This Listening section is similar to the Listening section you worked in Unit 1 at AS. It is therefore important that you remind yourself of the musical features that you learned to spot for that paper. You may also want to turn back to the Rhinegold Study Guide for AS music that you used last year. There (pages 7–18) you will find information on how to listen for and understand:

➤ Cadences – perfect, plagal, imperfect, interrupted

➤ Chord identification – primary triads, dominant 7th in root position, first and second inversions

➤ Modulations – to the subdominant, dominant and relative minor

➤ Melodic contour – intervals, passing notes, appoggiaturas, note of anticipation, trill, turn, mordent

➤ Metre – simple and compound time

➤ Textures – monophonic, homophonic, polyphonic

➤ Instrumentation

➤ Compositional devices – sequence, ostinato (or riff), canon, syncopation.

Here are some exercises to remind you of how these features sound. Use these in three ways:

➢ Play through them

➢ Study them through analysis

➢ Listen to them without watching the music by asking a friend to play them to you.

Exercise 1: cadence-spotting

Each even-numbered bar involves a cadence: can you identify what type it is?

Exercise 2: chord identification

This piece only uses chords I, IV, V and V^7, with each chord in root position or first or second inversion. Can you identify each chord?

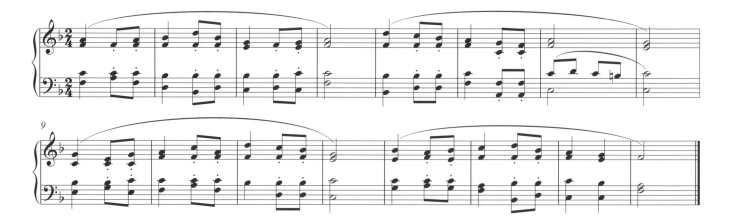

Now listen again and identify the four cadences in this piece.

Exercise 3: modulations

Here are three passages that modulate. Work out for each one whether the modulation is to the subdominant, dominant or relative minor.

You should also be able to identify two cadences in each of these passages (the first in the starting key and the second in the new key).

Exercise 4: melodic contour

Play, study and then listen to the following melody, and then answer the questions below:

1. Which note in bar 1 is a passing note? Why?

2. Which note in bar 2 is an appoggiatura? Why?

3. Where else are there appoggiaturas in the melodic line?

4. How would you describe the contour of the quavers in bars 3 and 7?

5. Which bar in the melody starts with an upward leap of a perfect 4th?

6. Which starts with an upward leap of a perfect 5th?

7. Which starts with an upward leap of a major 6th?

8. Which bar uses two notes of anticipation?

9. Where is there a sequence in the melody?

10. Where would be the most appropriate place for a trill to occur in this melody?

Exercise 5: metre

The following short piece comprises phrases that are in $\frac{6}{8}$, $\frac{4}{4}$, $\frac{3}{4}$, and $\frac{2}{4}$. The * sign indicates where a new metre begins. Identify each metre used.

If you work on this exercise with a friend, you should find that the first three phrases can be played in any order. Keep the same crotchet pulse throughout (so in $\frac{6}{8}$, quavers are the same speed as before).

Exercise 6: texture

Play and listen to the following piece and consider how best to describe the texture at each of the points indicated with brackets:

New material for A2

In addition to revising all these musical features and terms listed above that you met at AS, the A2 listening paper expects you to know a range of further technical details to which we can now turn.

In addition to the primary triads and dominant 7th chords that are required at AS, you need to be able to recognise some more advanced chords:

Advanced chord identification

➢ Diminished 7th chords

➢ Augmented 6th chords

➢ Secondary 7th chords

➢ Dominant 7th in third inversion (V^7d).

A diminished 7th chord can be formed from three intervals of a minor 3rd, stacked above each other. When written as shown in (a) on the next page, the interval between its outer notes is a diminished 7th, from which the chord takes its name. It often has a rather creepy or sinister sound. If the chord is inverted, as shown in (b), you will have to juggle the notes so that they are all on spaces (or all on lines) in order to see the diminished 7th. Inversion letters are not normally used when identifying this chord – it is enough to simply recognise it as a 'diminished 7th chord'.

The sound of the **diminished 7th chord** is very distinct, and should not prove too difficult to spot. More often than not it acts like 'dominant' to the following chord, creating a sense of resolution to the heightened tension that the diminished 7th induces. Alternatively the use of successive diminished 7th chords magnifies the uneasy character of the harmonic colour.

Exercise 7: diminished 7th chords

See if you can spot the diminished 7ths in the following passage, both by eye and ear.

Augmented 6th chords are curious beasts. Heard out of context they can sound exactly like dominant 7th chords. In a passage of tonal harmony, however, they cannot be mistaken for two reasons: the root of the chord, and the manner of resolution. Visually the chords stand out with the root and 6th 'spelled' to give an augmented 6th interval, instead of a minor 7th which is found in a dominant 7th chord. There are three varieties depending on what other notes are used 'inside' the chord:

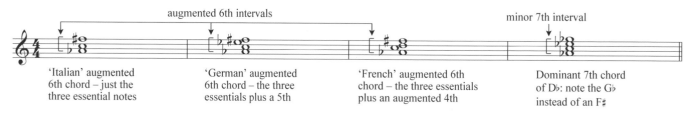

'Italian' augmented 6th chord – just the three essential notes

'German' augmented 6th chord – the three essentials plus a 5th

'French' augmented 6th chord – the three essentials plus an augmented 4th

Dominant 7th chord of Db: note the Gb instead of an F♯

Nearly all augmented 6th chords occur on the flattened sixth degree of the scale (in a minor key the 6th is already flattened); just occasionally they can be found on the flattened second degree. From the flattened sixth they resolve outwards onto the dominant, with either a dominant chord or chord Ic. From the flattened second the chord resolves onto the tonic.

Exercise 8: augmented 6th chords

There are several augmented 6th chords in this piece. Can you find them all and work out whether they are Italian, German or French versions?

Secondary 7th chords are chromatic chords. In any major key there are three major triads and three minor triads:

Clearly chord V^7 often leads to chord I, as occurs in a perfect cadence. However, each of the other five chords can, in turn, be introduced by their own 'dominant 7th chord'. This results in the use of various accidentals in the process, but without threatening the stability of the key or imposing a modulation on the music:

Exercise 9: secondary 7th chords

Compare these two versions of the same piece. The first only uses diatonic chords of C major; the second uses exactly the same chords in the same places but prefaces each chord with its secondary 7th on the last beat of the previous bar. Listen carefully to the difference when it is played, and note that the piece never leaves C major: it just has much more harmonic colour.

Inversions of a 7th chord:

Root of the chord in the bass = root position

3rd of the chord in the bass = first inversion

5th of the chord in the bass = second inversion

7th of the chord in the bass = third inversion.

The **dominant 7th chord in third inversion** is not such an exotic chord: you will have met many dominant 7th chords by now. Since any 7th chord comprises four different notes (rather than the three we find in a triad) there is an extra inversion available: if we have the 7th degree of the chord in the bass we will find the third inversion of the chord.

Whenever the dominant 7th is used, the natural choice of chord to have next is the tonic. In good part-writing the 7th itself naturally wants to fall onto the third degree of the tonic chord. If the dominant 7th is used in third inversion, the 7th is in the bass and this will lead to the tonic being used in first inversion.

With neither of these chords in root position and a small step of a semitone downwards in the bass, this makes for a pleasingly fluid progression. Secondary 7th chords can also be used in the same manner, i.e. in third inversion with the related diatonic chord taken in first inversion.

Exercise 10: dominant 7th in third inversion

The first chord of this piece is V^7d. Several secondary 7ths are taken in the same way. Can you locate them all, both by sight and aural perception?

Tonality

You will already feel confident telling the difference between music in a major or a minor key. The A2 specification also requires you to be able to tell the difference between **tonal, modal** and various kinds of **atonal** music, i.e. music that does not use a key.

You need to be familiar with four more kinds of musical language:

➤ Modality

➤ Atonality

➤ Music based on a whole-tone scale

➤ Bitonality.

Modality exists in many formats, but four important modes are worth your attention. These are the old church modes which were given new life in the 20th century by a range of musicians from Vaughan Williams to the Beatles.

These modes, like the major and minor scales, fit eight notes to the octave, but they differ in the placement of the two semitones within the scale. The result is the following four modal scales which are remembered most simply by thinking of 'white note' scales on a piano keyboard:

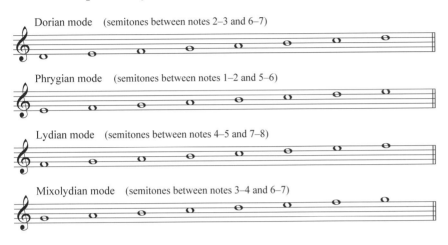

The higher up the scale these semitones occur, the brighter the resultant scale and music will sound; conversely, the lower they occur in the scale, the darker and more gloomy the resulting scale and music will sound. The following chart will show how this works out:

	1–2	2–3	3–4	4–5	5–6	6–7	7–8
Lydian mode				*			*
Major scale			*				*
Mixolydian mode			*			*	
Dorian mode		*				*	
Melodic minor (descending)		*			*		
Phrygian mode	*				*		

* = where semitones occur

Music written using these modes will not sound so different from tonal music: there are still eight notes to the octave, with a sense of keynote or tonic present. The chart suggests that music in the lydian mode will sound a little brighter than music in a major key, while music in the mixolydian mode will sound a little less bright than major key music. Similarly, music in the phrygian mode will sound darker than music in a minor key, while music in the dorian mode will sound a little less dark than minor key music.

Exercise 11: modality

Here are five phrases to play or listen to. Identify the modality or tonality of each.

Atonal music describes a type of harmony made famous by a group of composers called the Second Viennese School. These three composers – Arnold Schoenberg, Alban Berg and Anton Webern – experimented with increasingly dissonant harmonies and lessened the importance of the tonic and tonal hierarchy in their music. Later, they developed 12-note technique, in which all 12 notes of the chromatic scale are given equal importance, as a method for organising harmony.

Good works to listen to in order to become acquainted with this style include Schoenberg's Variations for Orchestra Op. 31 (1928), Berg's *Lyric* Suite (1926), and Webern's String Quartet Op. 28 (1938).

The following short excerpt will give you an initial impression of how strange-sounding this style can be:

Music based on a **whole-tone scale** was developed largely by the Impressionist composers in France, such as Debussy and Ravel, before becoming a tool of the composer's craft in the 20th century. Quite simply, whole-tone music makes use of a scale (there are only two: one starting on C, the other on C♯) that contains seven notes rather than eight in an octave, each one being a whole tone from its neighbouring notes:

There is an attractive 'other-worldly' quality to much whole-tone music, something rather haunting and hypnotic. An excellent first taste of this sound-world is Debussy's *Voiles* from his first book of Preludes (1910). Meanwhile, here is a short excerpt of whole-tone music to try:

Bitonality, as the word suggests, is music that uses two keys from the tonal system at the same time. As you might expect, the result is rather conflicted and grotesque; examples worth looking at include Charles Ives' setting of Psalm 67, a famous passage from Stravinsky's ballet *Petrushka* in which arpeggios of C major and F♯ major are set against each other, and the duet from the Prologue to Britten's opera *Peter Grimes*.

Pianists can have some fun experimenting with the left hand playing in one key, while the right plays in another. The results

Arnold Whittall wrote that 'the failure of bitonality to win wider acceptance confirms that it is a distinctly mechanical way of deriving something new from something traditional' *(New Grove, 2nd edition)*.

tend to be hit and miss, but here is one short example to set the ball rolling:

Modulation

At AS you had to be ready to spot modulations (changes of key) from a major tonic to the subdominant, dominant or relative minor. Now there are further possible modulations to look out for:

➢ From a major tonic to the tonic minor (C major to C minor)

➢ From a minor tonic to a minor dominant

➢ From a minor tonic to the relative major.

The first of these, from **tonic major to tonic minor**, you will already have met, for Beethoven does this in his first symphony – last year's set work. The change to minor tonality should feel instantly colder; when the music moves to the relative minor the change of tonic note can soften the change of major to minor, because there were indications that there was a change of key coming; but when the tonic remains the same the change can be very sudden, like an icy blast. Nearly always the way into the tonic minor is from the dominant chord, for the dominant chord is the same in a major key as it is in a minor key, allowing for this sudden change.

Moving from a **minor tonic to the minor dominant** is not so unlike the change from a major tonic to the dominant that you learned to spot at AS, except both keys are now minor. The dominant, being one degree sharper in terms of key signature, should seem somewhat higher in character, but colder too – like the ice box at the top of your fridge – since it is still minor.

The modulation from a **minor tonic to the relative major** should be easy to spot: there is an immediate sense of a warm, confident sound, as not only has the music gone from minor to major, but the tonic has moved upwards by a minor 3rd too.

Exercise 12: modulations

Identify (with eyes or ears) the relationship between the starting and finishing keys of each of these phrases:

Harmonic devices

The specification expects you to be able to spot four kinds of harmonic device:

➤ Pedal notes – tonic and dominant

➤ Cycle of 5ths progressions

➤ Suspensions

➤ Sequences.

Pedal notes are sustained or repeated pitches, often in the bass, while the harmony changes over the top. Spotting them should be easy; try to work out whether the pedal note is the tonic or the dominant. If it is the tonic the effect will be one of stability; if it is the dominant there will be a sense of building expectation, and at some point it will move forwards, most likely onto the tonic.

The **cycle of 5ths** progression has been a favoured pattern for composers since before the time of Bach. You met a particularly good example last year in the development section of the opening movement to Beethoven's Symphony No. 1. Other examples from more recent music include the jazz standard *Fly Me to the Moon*, Gloria Gaynor's hit song *I Will Survive* and Michael Nyman's *Time Lapse* from the 1985 film *A Zed and Two Noughts*.

Listen to some examples of the cycle of 5ths progression and try to sense the way that, once the pattern has started, there is almost unstoppable propulsion forwards.

Suspensions are among the oldest of all harmonic devices. There are various types, but they all share the same principle: the note from one chord is suspended over into the next chord, in

If you are studying Area of Study 3a 'English choral music in the 20th century', look out for the magnificent tonic pedal that lasts for much of the opening to the final movement of Howells' *Hymnus paradisi*.

which it creates a dissonance, before resolving onto a consonant note. The effect creates a dash of spice in the harmonic writing. Here are a few examples:

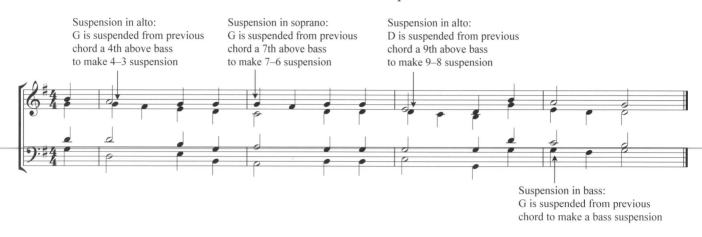

Suspension in alto:
G is suspended from previous chord a 4th above bass to make 4–3 suspension

Suspension in soprano:
G is suspended from previous chord a 7th above bass to make 7–6 suspension

Suspension in alto:
D is suspended from previous chord a 9th above bass to make 9–8 suspension

Suspension in bass:
G is suspended from previous chord to make a bass suspension

We have already covered **sequence** when applied to melodic ideas (see Exercise 4, page 10). Harmony too can contain sequential patterns where the move from chord 1 to chord 2 is copied at a different pitch for chords 3 to 4. For this reason, the cycle of 5ths progression is one common way of generating sequence in the harmony (for example moving from chord VI to II sets the pattern for the next two chords – V to I – which have a similar relationship).

Exercise 13: harmonic devices

Play and listen to the following piece and locate each of the following:

1. A dominant pedal and a tonic pedal
2. A phrase with several suspensions
3. A passage of cycle of 5ths harmony
4. A phrase with a different harmonic sequence to the first
5. Chord V^7 in 3rd inversion.

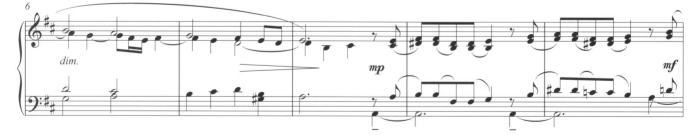

More metres

The more common metres have already been covered in Exercise 5, page 10. At A2 you may also meet music with either five or seven beats in a bar. These should not be difficult to spot: they tend to have a somewhat lopsided effect since in both cases the bar subdivides into asymmetric halves. The best preparation is to listen to some examples:

Five beats in a bar

➢ Tchaikovsky: 3rd movement, Symphony No. 6 *(Pathétique)*

➢ Holst: 'Mars' from the *Planets* Suite

➢ Brubeck: *Take Five.*

Seven beats in a bar

➢ Stravinsky: 'Final Hymn' from the *Firebird*

➢ Britten: 'Dies irae' from *War Requiem* (see page 90)

➢ Brubeck: *Unsquare Dance.*

Hemiola

Hemiola is a particular rhythmic device that is sometimes found in music that is in triple time ($\frac{3}{4}$). Triple time usually lends music an elegant 'lilting' feel, with the first beat of the bar given more stress than the other two. In hemiola this pattern is disrupted with alternate beats stressed over a period of two bars. This gives the impression that three bars of duple time have replaced two bars of triple time, and is often used to give weight to a cadence pattern.

Sometimes the hemiola is apparent from the rhythm in the melodic line; more often it is the change of harmonic rhythm which pinpoints the presence of hemiola.

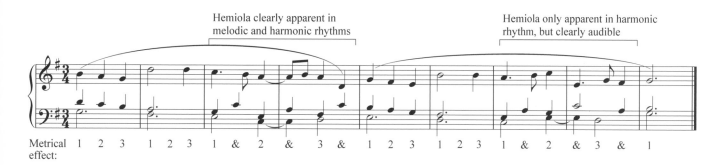

Section B: Area of Study 1

Introduction

Area of Study 1 involves studying a set work. You can choose between two symphonies written in the 20th century: Elgar's Symphony No. 1 in A♭ major (1907), and Shostakovich's Symphony No. 5 in D major (1937). One or both of these set works could change for exams in June 2016, or may even change earlier, so you should always check carefully the up-to-date AQA specification.

For the symphony you choose to study, you will find a matching set of questions in Section B of the exam paper. There will be two shorter essays to write on specific details in selected passages from the piece (each worth 10 marks), as well as a longer essay for which you have a choice of two questions, of which you answer only one. Questions will require you to discuss the composer's approach to the main elements of composition: melody, harmony and tonality, rhythm and metre, texture, instrumentation and timbre, and structure. It is also a good idea to know something of the historical context of the symphony, both in terms of the composer's life and the wider influences of the time.

Both symphonies are substantial pieces. The playing time of the Elgar is around 55 minutes; the Shostakovich is nearer to 45 minutes. Whichever one you choose to study will require regular listening and study if you are to become familiar with all its music in time for the exam. Try to find a live performance of the piece to attend as well: this is likely to make a much deeper impression on you than just relying on repeated listening to the CD. In large-scale and complex works such as these, it is remarkable how much more we notice when we can watch the music being played. So treat yourself to a night out at a concert – one of the real perks of doing an A level in music!

A brief history of the symphony

At AS you studied Beethoven's Symphony No. 1 (1800). By the time the 19th century turned into the 20th, the symphony had evolved into a much bigger work. However beautiful and uplifting the music of Beethoven's first symphony, there remains a sense that in 1800 a symphony was primarily for entertainment. The Romantic era saw the symphony as a vehicle for saying something profound about the human experience: an altogether different role for composers to explore.

After his first symphony, Beethoven made the first break with the Classical view of the symphony in his Symphony No. 3. Also known as the *Eroica*, the work lasts about 50 minutes and, as the title suggests, has something rather more substantial than entertainment as its inspiration. It was a watershed piece in the history of music, which established a new symphonic 'ideal'. For the first time there is a sense that a symphony takes the listener on a journey of psychological growth – perhaps even a spiritual journey. Beethoven further explored this potential in his fifth, sixth and seventh symphonies, and above all in his ninth (which involves singers in the final movement).

Following in Beethoven's footsteps in the Austro-German tradition, Brahms and Bruckner further increased the scope of the symphony. Then came Mahler, who took the genre to a new level of complexity and scale of concept. For example, Mahler's second *Resurrection* symphony explores a deeply spiritual theme, engaging the listener with overwhelming emotional force.

As the scope increased, so too did the challenge of writing symphonies. Haydn wrote 104 symphonies, Mozart 41, but to 19th-century composers each symphony was a huge undertaking: Brahms only wrote four and Bruckner nine, for instance. Each movement needed more material and more development; one theme would not suffice for a first subject. The term 'first-subject group' is used where a collection of ideas comprise the first-subject area. With more ideas, the development sections become more complex too.

In the late Romantic era, composers from more countries took up the challenge of writing symphonies. By the middle of the 20th century, symphonies were being written from Russia to America, and from Finland to Brazil. The symphony became more diverse: Sibelius' seventh symphony is written in one continuous movement; Mahler's third has six movements. However, four movements remained the standard format (to which both A2 set works comply).

The Romantic orchestra

One of the factors in the increasing weight and emotional range of the 19th-century symphony was the development in instruments. For much of the Classical period the orchestra comprised two oboes, two bassoons, two horns and a small group of strings. Sometimes there would be a flute; trumpets and timpani might appear if the music was in a 'brass-friendly' key such as C or D. (All brass instruments were limited by a lack of valves, so only notes of the harmonic series were available.) Late in the 18th century the clarinet was developed, and by Haydn's last symphonies (and Beethoven's first) the woodwind section was properly established: eight players, two each of flutes, oboes, clarinets and bassoons, otherwise known as 'double woodwind'. Even then, as you will remember from AS, in the slow movement of his first symphony Beethoven does not use the second flute.

During the 19th century the orchestra continued to develop at a rapid rate; composers such as Berlioz and Richard Strauss were quick to push the limits of all instruments in their orchestral works. The main developments were:

➢ **Brass** – trombones first used in Beethoven's fifth; two tubas used by Berlioz in *Symphonie fantastique*; four horns became standard with Beethoven and Brahms, with more appearing in the later 19th century; the development of the valve for horns

If you go to see a live performance of your set work, count the horn players carefully, as there may well be five. This is because the demands of playing first horn in symphonies of this scale are so onerous that it is customary to share the part between two players. The back-up player is known as the 'bumper'.

and trumpets gave these instruments a fully chromatic range, which meant composers could use them in any key.

➢ **Woodwind** – double woodwind section gradually evolved into triple or even quadruple woodwind; extra players often doubled on alternative instruments including piccolo, cor anglais, the small E♭ clarinet, bass clarinet and contrabassoon.

➢ **Strings** – the section grew in size to balance enlarged wind sections; 16 first violins, 14 second violins, 12 violas, ten cellos, and eight double basses became the Romantic orchestra norm; a wider range used on all string instruments (going much higher); cellos became emancipated from playing the bass line for much of the time due to other possibilities in the orchestra.

➢ **Percussion** – timpani became a more regular feature, along with other instruments such as cymbals, bass drum, snare drum, etc.; by the 20th century all manner of other instruments such as xylophone, glockenspiel and so on available.

➢ **Other** – the harp was used more often by the time of the late Romantics; piano, organ and other keyboard instruments such as the celeste occasionally used.

The table below lists the orchestras employed by Elgar and Shostakovich.

	Elgar Symphony No. 1	Shostakovich Symphony No. 5
Woodwind		
Flutes	3 (one doubling piccolo)	2 + 1 piccolo
Oboes	2 + 1 cor anglais	2
Clarinets	2 + 1 bass clarinet	2 + 1 E♭ clarinet
Bassoons	2 + 1 contrabassoon	2 + 1 contrabassoon
Brass		
Horns	4	4
Trumpets	3	3
Trombones	3	3
Tubas	1	1
Percussion	Timpani, snare drum, bass drum, cymbals (4 players in all)	Timpani, snare drum, bass drum, cymbals (including a suspended cymbal), triangle, xylophone, glockenspiel (5 players in all)
Strings	Full complement of 16.14.12.10.8	Full complement of 16.14.12.10.8
Other	2 harps	2 harps; piano and celeste (1 player)
TOTAL	99 players	100 players

The large orchestras employed by Elgar and Shostakovich include more transposing instruments than you had to handle in the Beethoven AS set work. The rule remains the same, however: the note in the title is what you hear when the instrument plays a written C. There is one extra catch: the cor anglais is always 'in F' but is rarely stated as such; you can tell by looking at its written key signature. Therefore, you need to be aware of the following transpositions:

➢ Clarinet in B♭ sounds a tone *lower* than written

➢ Clarinet in A sounds a minor 3rd *lower* than written

➢ Clarinet in E♭ sounds a minor 3rd *higher* than written

➢ Cor anglais in F sounds a perfect 5th *lower* than written

➢ Horn in F sounds a perfect 5th *lower* than written

➢ Trumpet in B♭ sounds a tone *lower* than written.

Transposing instruments

In addition:
- Bass clarinet sounds an extra octave *lower* than written (in addition to the tone or minor 3rd transposition)

- The piccolo sounds an octave *higher* than written

- The contrabassoon sounds an octave *lower* than written

- When a horn in F is written in bass clef, it sounds a perfect 4th *higher* than written (instead of a perfect 5th lower)

- Double basses sound an octave *lower* than written.

Elgar: Symphony No. 1

The composer

Edward Elgar (1857–1934) was the composer who (after a long drought following the death of Purcell in 1695) gave an international profile to British music. His achievement is all the more remarkable given that he was essentially self-taught as a composer. The previous generation of English composers, such as Stanford and Parry, had written symphonies. However, their works were overshadowed by the major composers of continental Europe – figures such as Brahms, Dvořák or Tchaikovsky.

Elgar, born in a village close to Worcester, spent many years developing his skills and musical experiences. He studied scores from his father's music shop as a boy, and earned his living as a young man by teaching violin, playing in the Three Choirs Festival at Worcester in 1884, and directing the band at the local Powick Lunatic Asylum. Gradually more of his time was spent composing; early works include the delightful *Serenade for Strings* (1892) and various pieces written for choral societies, such as his oratorio *Caractacus* (1898).

Two works at the turn of the century brought Elgar to national and international fame: his orchestral *Enigma Variations* (1899) and oratorio *The Dream of Gerontius* (1900). Subsequently, Elgar's works brought him many honours in his lifetime and a highly respected place in history.

You may be studying *The Dream of Gerontius* as part of your Area of Study 3a. There is some information on it on page 76.

Many would say that Elgar's greatest compositional skill was his ability to exploit the full range of colour of the late Romantic orchestra. For example, in *The Dream of Gerontius*, although there are two wonderful solo singing roles (for Gerontius and the Angel), and some thrilling passages for the chorus to sing, it is often the orchestral writing that gives the music its rich, emotional power. Following the success of his oratorio, it would only be a matter of time, therefore, before Elgar would be drawn to tackle the most important of orchestral genres: the symphony.

Elgar worked on his first symphony between 1907–08. Following its premiere by the Hallé Orchestra, in Manchester on 3 December 1908, it was an immediate success – more so than any other of his works. He was called to the platform after the first movement, and again after the third movement, and then five times at the end of the performance. In just over a year the symphony had received its 100th performance, and had been played across Europe, and in America and Australia.

Elgar's second symphony followed in 1911; many think it is an even more profound piece than his first, although initially it was not so well received. After the death of his wife in 1920, Elgar virtually stopped composing. Then in the early 1930s he was commissioned by the BBC to write a new symphony. A large number of sketches were made, however Elgar stopped work upon being diagnosed with cancer, and he died in 1934. The composer Anthony Payne worked over many years to piece together 130 pages of Elgar's sketches. Subsequently, a work known as 'Edward Elgar: the sketches for Symphony No. 3, elaborated by Anthony Payne' was finally given a premiere in 1998, fittingly by the BBC Symphony Orchestra. The construction makes a fascinating coda to Elgar's symphonic music.

Symphony No. 1

Completed in 1908, Elgar follows the standard four-movement pattern for a late Romantic symphony:

> First movement: a fast movement (see Allegro at fig. 5) with a slow introduction (Andante. Nobilmente e semplice)

> Second movement: another fast movement with the character of a scherzo (Allegro molto)

> Third movement: the slow movement (Adagio)

> Fourth movement: a fast finale (begins Lento, after fig. 111 Allegro).

The structural planning behind Elgar's symphony is remarkably elaborate. The central two movements are closely related and are intended to be played without the customary break between movements. More significantly, the first melody line that we hear at the start of the work returns at the end of the whole symphony in a technique sometimes called 'cyclic form'. Previous examples of such a technique include Tchaikovsky's fifth symphony and César Franck's Symphony in D minor, both written in 1888.

Scores: there are good editions of the study score for this symphony published by Novello and Eulenberg. Elgar wrote numerical rehearsal marks into his score at regular intervals; these will be used to identify locations in the analysis that follows.

Recordings: there are many high-quality recordings of Elgar's Symphony No. 1 available on the market. Of particular interest is the recording of Elgar himself conducting the symphony, made in 1930 (Naxos). Of the more recent recordings, you may want to check out the performance of the modern-day Hallé Orchestra under Sir Mark Elder.

In the 18th-century symphony (as in Beethoven's first symphony) the slow movement is placed second. However, in the 19th century, it was more common for composers to put the slow movement third, at the 'heart' of the symphony; Beethoven's ninth symphony is a famous early example of this practice.

First movement: Andante

The first movement of the Beethoven symphony studied at AS has a playing time of around 9 minutes, which includes a straightforward repeat of the exposition. The first movement of Elgar's Symphony No. 1 is approximately 20 minutes. Therefore, expect a greater degree of complexity.

You will know the main sections of sonata form from your study of Beethoven:

Preliminary matters

Introduction	Exposition	Development	Recapitulation	Coda
An optional section (usually a slow passage to start the movement)	First subject (tonic) Transition Second subject (dominant) Codetta (dominant)	Material presented in the exposition is explored while the music passes through various keys (avoiding the tonic)	First subject (tonic) Transition Second subject (tonic) Codetta (tonic)	A rounding off to the movement (primarily tonic)

When a sonata-form movement is written in a minor key, there is an alternative key scheme that the composer can use as a standard practice: the exposition can move to the relative major for the second subject instead of the dominant key. This then has the implication that, whereas the first subject is intrinsically minor by character, the second subject is major; in the recapitulation, therefore, the music changes to the tonic major for the reappearance of the second subject. A clear example of this (despite some modification to the recapitulation of the first subject) can be seen in the first movement of Haydn's Symphony No. 80 in D minor. The keys visited here are:

You may like to remind yourself of these main sections by listening again to the first movement of Beethoven's Symphony No. 1.

Exposition		Development	Recapitulation	
First subject	Second subject		First subject	Second subject
D minor	F major	various	D minor	D major

Overview

Elgar constructs his first movement according to established sonata-form principles, with the various sections in the expected order:

Section	Figures	Comprising
Introduction (Andante)	Bar 1 up to fig. 5	
Exposition	Fig. 5 (Allegro) to fig. 19	First subject: from third bar of fig. 5
		Second subject: from fig. 12
		Codetta: from fig. 18
Development	Fig. 19 to 32	
Recapitulation	Fig. 32 to 48	First subject: from fig. 32
		Second subject: from fig. 38
Coda	Fig. 48 to end of movement (after fig. 55)	

As you listen to and study the music with which Elgar fills this symphonic structure, you will find a movement of considerable ingenuity and originality.

In his book *Elgar Orchestral Music*, part of the old BBC Music Guides series (published 1970), Elgar scholar Michael Kennedy recounts that the vintage Elgar conductor Sir Adrian Boult was told that a friend of Elgar's had made a bet he could not compose a symphony that was in two keys at the same time. Whatever the authenticity of that story, there is a fascinating dual polarity of tonal centres at work in Elgar's first symphony, which can be simplified to the following chart:

Introduction	First subject	Second subject	Development	First subject	Second subject	Coda
A♭ major	D minor	F major	various	D minor	A♭ major	A♭ major

This symphony is famous for being the only symphony in the regular orchestral repertoire in A♭ major. However, while the first movement begins and ends in that key, much of the inner workings of the movement seem to relate more to D minor. The two keys are utterly opposed to one another: one major, the other minor; and D is exactly half an octave (or a tritone) away from A♭. (Compare the chart above with the one on the previous page for Haydn's Symphony No. 80 in D minor.)

Introduction: start to fig. 5

The opening passage is quite substantial to be called an 'Introduction', being around 3'30" in duration. After two distant timpani rolls, it presents a long and expansive melody that is usually known as the 'motto' theme. (In contrast, another famous symphony of the period, Rachmaninov's second, has a motto theme comprising just seven notes.) Elgar's motto theme reappears several times during the first movement, and then it returns in a rich orchestral texture to round off the whole symphony.

The theme comes in two asymmetric phrases. The first, lasting seven bars, ends with an imperfect cadence and contains some important characteristics: a largely conjunct contour save for a few typically Elgarian leaps such as the rising 6th between the fourth and fifth notes, and a gentle rhythmic nature with some lingering ties held over the barlines:

The second phrase (fig. 1–2) begins the same way, but expands on the first by being of considerably greater length (16 bars), and by rising higher. It ends on the tonic.

The texture and orchestration of the passage is of considerable interest and points to a composer with a fine imagination for tone colour. The melody is carried by an unusual blend: clarinets and violas in octaves, a flute doubling the upper octave and a bassoon the lower one. The result is tender, expressive and distinctive. For the most part, the only accompaniment is a bass line of staccato crotchets played by the cellos and double basses. This creates a distant suggestion of a march – in keeping with Elgar's favourite 'nobilmente' marking – while the resulting restrained texture suggests the 'semplice' instruction. Between fig. 1 and 2 there are two short phrases on muted horns that provide a touch of harmony.

This only accounts for half the introduction, however. Elgar then restates the theme in its entirety at fig. 3, tutti and *ff*. The melody is carried by the first violins and flutes, with the warm sound of the horns in support. The trombones are important in providing the harmony in a rich tenor register. The marching bass line is played not just by the low strings, but also by bassoons and tuba.

> Listen out for the detail of timpani and harp in the texture: especially the marvellous *p* to *f* drum roll in the second bar of fig. 3.

After fig. 4, the full orchestral sound melts away until the motto theme ends with a scoring very similar to how it was first heard at the start. The bass line ends with the following sequential pattern (one of Elgar's most fond techniques):

The harmony of this opening section is almost entirely diatonic. There is one small inflection of a secondary dominant (chord V of V, i.e. B♭ major) in the sixth bar after fig. 3. The result is that the opening 3½ minutes of the symphony are tonally stable, and the long, lyrical melody line creates a luxurious feel in the rich key of A♭ major. What follows is highly contrasting.

> Do not be fooled by the accidentals in the transposing horn parts. These are written according to an old convention where no key signature is used.

Exposition: fig. 5 to 19

First-subject area: fig. 5–12

When the tempo changes to Allegro, the character of the symphony changes completely. There is a sense of D minor – as already mentioned, a key far removed from A♭ major – as outlined at the start of the new melodic theme in the first violins:

The Roman numerals above the first violin stave indicate which string the violins should use. Elgar requests playing in a high position on a low string to gain a passionate tone quality.

Julian Rushton's essay in *The Cambridge Companion to Elgar* says of the first subject 'whilst not exactly atonal, it belongs to no single key' (Cambridge University Press, 2005).

The tonality is now far less stable, with frequent accidentals in both the melody and the harmony. The latter makes no use of the tonality-clinching dominant 7th chord. In further contrast to the motto theme, the melodic line is largely disjunct; more so after fig. 6. The texture and orchestration is more elaborate, and the dynamic markings (with frequent accents and sforzandos) complete the tempestuous character.

From fig. 7 to 8 the rising melodic line is set over a descending bass line that creates an expanding texture. The accompaniment creates enormous energy and momentum by playing on beats two and four. Very few of these accompanying chords are in root position, and many are forms of various 7th chords. These elements all add to a sense of propulsion; as it reaches a pinnacle at fig. 8, the first-subject theme starts again, this time in the tenor register on the cellos and horns.

From fig. 8 the sense of build-up includes rising demisemiquaver flourishes alternately on the harp and violins. As the climax is reached at fig. 9, the metre changes to a compound ⁶₄ time signature with a rising and falling figure on the horns, which is immediately contradicted by a ³₂ feel in the violin melody. This is, again, a sequential pattern:

At fig. 10 the ³₂ feel against the ⁶₄ metre continues in parallel 10ths. The scoring employs an unusual blend of second violins divisi, with violas supporting the top part and cellos the lower line:

This marks the beginning of a transition passage in which the music subsides. The first violins introduce a new idea at fig. 11, which has more of the compound feel:

The new idea in fig. 11 moves away from an unstable minor tonality and cadences into F major at fig. 12.

The second subject (at least initially) returns to a more diatonic style. However, a sense of metrical complexity is created by the melody being in $\frac{2}{2}$ while the accompaniment continues to be in the compound $\frac{6}{4}$ until fig. 13. The legato melodic idea in the first violins at fig. 12 appears to be in distinct contrast to the stormy first-subject idea. However, on closer inspection, the fourth and eighth bars suggest an inversion of the first subject's opening gesture, the rhythm being particularly telling:

A delicate accompaniment avoids including the bass-register instruments and there are arabesque-like figures in the second violin and flute.

At fig. 13, the second subject is restated in a tenor register through a sonorous combination of cellos, horn, bassoon and clarinet. The first violins then explore briefly the idea in an indeterminate flat key, maybe D♭ major or B♭ minor; there is no affirming cadence.

At fig. 14, Elgar reverts to the compound-time music that he introduced as transition material in fig. 10. The music surges forwards urgently, not least through heavy emphasis of the weak beats when the orchestra returns to $\frac{2}{2}$ time towards fig. 15. It is much more chromatic in harmonic vocabulary than when the second subject was first presented in fig. 12. Although still in the exposition, there is a flavour of development – especially with rhythmically augmented appearances of the opening to the first subject in the flutes, nine and six bars before fig. 15.

The full orchestral tutti builds towards fig. 16. At this point a four-quaver pattern is passed downwards through the strings, which heralds another brief reappearance of the first subject's opening D minor triadic shape. This leads to a melodic idea at fig. 17, which is dominated by all four horns in unison and marked *fff*. This is a new closing theme to the exposition. However, Elgar has already made use of the idea in the clarinet and violins five bars after fig. 11. At fig. 17 the idea is rhythmically augmented. As the force of this idea subsides, the music cadences at fig. 18 into C major.

The close of the exposition is marked by a short reappearance of the motto theme, played by muted horns and discreetly supported by tremolando violas. The cellos and double basses again have the staccato marching bass line; a little harmony is provided by the first flute and first bassoon, doubling in octaves.

Exercise 14

1. Which instruments play in the first bar of the symphony?

2. How many layers are there to the texture of the music up to fig. 3?

3. Which instruments are played muted before fig. 3?

4. What do the Roman numerals above the violin staves indicate?

5. What evidence is there to suggest that the Allegro after fig. 5 is in D minor?

6. What effects does Elgar use to create a sense of momentum in his music between fig. 7 and 9?

7. In what ways does the second subject at fig. 12 contrast with the first-subject material?

8. To what extent can the music between fig. 14 and 17 be seen as developmental in character?

Development: fig. 19–32

Throughout the development, Elgar continually blends thematic fragments from the exposition with new material. Coupled with his heavily chromatic harmonic vocabulary and constantly changing textures and orchestration, the music is quite challenging to analyse.

An overall sense of structure is given by a simple arch-shape that builds in texture, dynamic and intensity to the passage at fig. 27, and then subsides towards the recapitulation. Below are significant details to listen out for in each figure.

Fig. 19: a new melodic idea in the first violins starts with a rising 5th (possibly taken from the bass part 13 and 15 bars after fig. 8), and continues with a conjunct (and at times chromatic) descent. Its answering phrase allows the leaps to become more significant and wider, as seen in the example below:

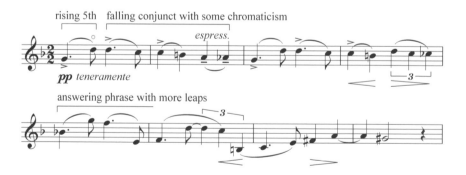

This leaping melody, coupled with the juxtaposition of an accompaniment largely in triplet crotchets, creates a sense of agitation – notwithstanding the **pp** dynamic marking. It is worth noting the shape in the cello part in the third bar after fig. 19, which will be significant in the texture of the accompaniment over the next few phrases, and is possibly derived from the closing theme of the exposition back at fig. 17.

Fig. 20: a similar passage using the same new melodic idea of fig. 19, but now more lavishly scored. Note the use of octave divisi doublings in the strings, and how the answering phrase is shared by half the violas and half the cellos in the middle of the texture.

Fig. 21: the metre changes to the compound $\frac{6}{4}$ (anticipated by the triplet crotchets that pass from the strings to the clarinets at this point). The woodwind play the transition idea first presented at fig. 10. A few bars later the winds adopt a quaver pattern reminiscent of the flute arabesques from the second subject at fig. 12. The string writing leading into fig. 22 is very detailed: tremolando second violins and violas played sul ponticello (bowing at the bridge, to create a ghostly timbre), with pizzicato first violins and cellos playing divisi; accents and *sfp* add to the precision of Elgar's writing.

Fig. 22: there is a sense of B minor now, with a B pedal note (cellos, timpani and horn) five bars after fig. 22. There is a kaleidoscopic mix of melodic shapes, including the arabesque quavers and the transition idea from fig. 9 (for example, horns in the third bar of fig. 22).

Fig. 23: the transition theme from fig. 11 is now given prominence and passed around the orchestra, starting in the wind and set against rising chromatic patterns in the strings. This soon gathers confidence and the music surges to *ff* by the fifth bar, but just as quickly subsides towards fig. 24.

Fig. 24 and 25: these passages are dominated by a new melodic shape of considerable angularity. In its first bar, the melody combines a rising perfect 5th (possibly related to the theme at fig. 19) and a rising 6th (perhaps from the start of the motto theme). The second bar includes a trademark Elgarian falling 7th:

The chromaticism of the idea defies any easy tonal analysis. However, there is a sense of passing from a tonal centre of B to one of B♭ four bars after fig. 24. This shift marks the start of a sustained passage of building intensity and complexity, which will reach its pinnacle at fig. 28.

Fig. 26: the whole orchestra now becomes involved with the symphonic intensity of the development. For a few bars there is another pedal B in the timpani, trombone and double basses. However, the overall tonality is highly unstable with considerable chromaticism across the elaborate texture. Melodic lines include some upward-thrusting angular shapes (often involving 5ths) and falling chromatic conjunct patterns. The weaker second and fourth crotchets in the bar are often accented, adding to the sense of forward propulsion.

Fig. 27: marked 'Poco animato', the music is now quite frenzied. There are two main strands to the texture: displaced minims (tied across the barlines) in the upper registers, which echo the cross-rhythm of the transition idea from fig. 9; and an upward-thrusting, leaping bass line. Seven bars after fig. 27 this texture inverts.

Fig. 28: over an F♯ pedal note (with strong implications of being a dominant pedal in B minor once more), the second subject is presented in a new guise: minor tonality, *ff* and tempestuous. Initially heard on the richly blended timbre of oboe, cor anglais, clarinet and viola, with first horn joining a bar later, the theme is heard several times, with fragments in the trumpets at the height of this passionate passage. Eventually the tumult subsides, with the timpani roll fading to *pp*.

Fig. 29: the strange angular idea from fig. 24 returns, but it is now rhythmically augmented into minims. The extreme dynamics – *pp* to *fff* and back again within five bars – match the surging rise and fall of the melody. The harp, aided first by the oboe and then the cellos, plays a falling pattern reminiscent of fig. 16. As Elgar slips back into $\frac{6}{4}$ time for four bars, a solo violin has a three-note motif. It is a sighing gesture that features a rising 6th (possibly from the motto theme), which is treated to a rising sequence. Quaver patterns woven into the texture suggest the arabesque idea.

Fig. 30: much of this passage follows the same formula as fig. 29. However, the music is extended with further use of the transition material from fig. 10. Then, as the music reverts to $\frac{3}{2}$ time, a distant reference to the motto theme from the introduction is heard *pp* on a combination of clarinet, bassoon and cello. There is also a skeleton version of the detached marching bass line, now played pizzicato by the basses and half of the cellos.

Fig. 31: the final passage of the development returns to the new theme that was presented as the development began (fig. 19), now with a touch of the compound rhythms that featured elsewhere. Four bars before the recapitulation starts at fig. 32, this theme is played on the solo bass clarinet. It then is taken up by the cellos, which continue with it after the recapitulation has started, thereby smoothing over this major structural join.

Exercise 15

1. Describe the difference in texture between the music at fig. 19 and fig. 20.

2. What is the connection between the music at fig. 24 and fig. 29?

3. Which instruments play the second-subject theme between fig. 28 and 29?

4. Which passages in the development make use of pedal notes?

5. Discuss the balance between simple time and compound time within the development.

Recapitulation: fig. 32–48

The recapitulation for the most part follows the plan of the exposition. Up to fig. 35, the main melodic line remains identical, though Elgar indulges in various differences in orchestration. With the need for a different key for the second subject in mind, Elgar takes a change of direction at fig. 35, but at fig. 36 uses music based on fig. 9. Now back in compound time, the transition material meanders for a while before reaching A♭ major at fig. 38 – the key in which the motto was heard at the start of the movement. At this point the second subject is reintroduced, as in the exposition, by the first violins. Its second statement at fig. 39 is again more richly scored (compare to fig. 13). The music then builds thrillingly to another powerful appearance of the closing theme at fig. 44 (see fig. 17) before the recapitulation subsides to the start of the coda at fig. 48.

Coda: fig. 48 to end of movement (after fig. 55)

The coda is a substantial section to this symphonic movement, almost 4 minutes in length. It comprises three subsections as follows.

The start of the coda is built around a restatement of the motto theme in its entirety. However, it is reintroduced in the most subtle of ways at fig. 48: played by the back desk of first and second violins, violas and cellos, who then play divisi to create an octave doubling. With these eight players sat as a single arc of musicians at the back of the string section, it sounds very distant and almost ghostly. Meanwhile, the remainder of the strings refer back to the development theme from fig. 19, now in compound-time rhythms. Gradually more and more of the orchestra take up the motto theme, until at fig. 51 it sounds confident and assertive. It then quickly melts away as Elgar avoids a grand ending to this movement.

Fig. 48 to the ninth bar after fig. 51

This passage is a good example of why it is always better to hear a live performance: your headphones or speakers are not likely to give you the depth of sound needed to experience the true effect of the back desks playing at this point.

The theme that began the development is reintroduced, and the tonal stability of the previous passage is eroded as chromaticism returns to the harmonic writing. The texture becomes more of a tapestry, with various melodic ideas that dominated the development now returning (for instance the angular shape at fig. 52). With the dynamics remaining very soft, the passage is akin to remembering the development as if it were a dream.

Ninth bar after fig. 51 to fig. 54

Very delicately, the motto theme returns (flute, clarinet and muted horn), but the echoes of the development persist too (also *pp*) with the quaver arabesques. Finally the closing theme (heard originally in fig. 17) is played at fig. 55. The unusual final cadence has the bass moving from D♮ to A♭ : the two competing tonal centres of the whole movement, and a fitting way to finish the movement.

Fig. 54 to the end

1. What key centres are used for the recapitulation?

2. How does Elgar hide the return of the motto theme at fig. 48?

3. In what ways is the central section of the coda (from nine bars after fig. 51 to fig. 54):

   ➤ Similar to the development?

   ➤ Different to the development?

4. In what ways is the final passage of the movement from fig. 55 a suitable rounding off to this opening movement?

Second movement: Allegro molto

Overview

At around 7 minutes in duration, the second movement is the shortest of Elgar's Symphony No. 1. However, there is no shortage of notes involved as the music rushes by in an unusual $\frac{3}{2}$ time signature (one minim beat per bar). There are three main musical ideas that comprise the movement:

➤ A scherzo idea: a 'moto perpetuo' (perpetual motion) melody, which scurries along in staccato semiquavers and traverses a wide range – first heard at the start.

➤ A march idea: a melody that starts with three repeating marcato crotchets followed by a wide upwards leap, and continues with martial dotted rhythms – first heard at fig. 59.

➤ A trio idea: a rather more naïve or dainty melody that comprises mainly quavers, which seems content to explore a rather narrower range – first heard at fig. 66.

Elgar fashions these three constituent ideas into a fast-paced movement that has elements of traditional scherzo and trio (a standard middle movement form for a symphony), sonata form and even rondo. The main structure is as follows:

The classical definition of sonata rondo form is as follows:

- A: tonic ⎫
- B: dominant ⎬ akin to exposition (though the return to I departs from standard sonata form)
- A: tonic ⎭

- C: various keys (usually starting in opposite mode – major/minor – to A and B sections) – akin to development

- A: tonic ⎫
- B: tonic ⎬ akin to exposition
- A: tonic ⎭

- Coda: tonic.

Figure	Musical material	Scherzo and trio	Rondo	Sonata form
			If viewed as:	
Start	Scherzo (F♯ minor)	Scherzo	Rondo theme (A)	Exposition: First subject in I
57	Scherzo (secondary idea)	↓	↓	Transition
59	March (C♯ minor)	↓	First episode (B)	Second subject in V
64	Scherzo (F♯ minor)	↓	Rondo theme (A)	Codetta (but in I)
66	Trio (B♭ major)	Trio	Second episode (C)	In lieu of the development, exploring a 'distant' key
71	Scherzo (F♯ minor)	Scherzo	Rondo theme (A)	Recapitulation: First subject in I
72	Scherzo (secondary idea)	↓	↓	Transition
73	March (F♯ minor)	↓	Third episode (D)	Second subject in I
75	Scherzo	↓	Rondo (A)	Codetta
77	Trio (B♭ major)	Coda	Coda	Coda
82	Scherzo (F♯ minor)	↓	↓	↓
85	Trio (B♭ major)	↓	↓	↓
86	Scherzo (D♭ major to F♯ minor)	↓	↓	↓
87	Scherzo (D major to F♯ minor)	↓	↓	↓
90	March (F♯ minor)	↓	↓	↓

Based on the evidence in the table above, it seems most appropriate to define the movement as sonata rondo form, with the principal idea (the skittish semiquavers) having a strong scherzo character.

Exposition: start of movement to fig. 66

Strings, bassoons and timpani initiate a pulsing F♯ heard on alternate downbeats. Intervening bars have a quiet motif on lower strings, but one with considerable nervous energy:

First subject: start of movement to fig. 57

Note the meticulous bowing, articulation and dynamic markings that Elgar indicates. Violas, cellos, and half the basses play this figure, doubled across three octaves.

At the fifth bar, the first violins enter with the main scherzo theme, a virtually continuous flow of staccato semiquavers traversing nearly two octaves in a giddy fashion:

The two bracketed groups of semiquavers in the example above are combined with a little alteration (including augmenting the note values into quavers) to make the woodwind phrase that leads into fig. 56:

This technique of rhythmic augmentation is going to be very significant in the coda to the movement.

Given the more obvious connections between movements of this symphony (such as the motto theme), it is tempting to see these two bracketed shapes as relating to the first movement: the triad reminds us of the first subject in the Allegro, and the second shape is like the motif at fig. 16.

At fig. 56 the opening music is repeated with some slight changes of orchestration. These include the first three bars of the melody being doubled at the upper octave, adding a touch of luminosity to the music. The woodwind phrase is doubled to lead into fig. 57.

Transition: fig. 57–59

The transition is built from two ideas:

1. A brittle, angular pattern on the strings in which first violins and violas form a unison team, and second violins and cellos form another.

2. A pattern of four descending conjunct quavers, treated sequentially, that hark back – albeit in a much more animated fashion – to the first four notes of the motto theme.

This passage is played twice, and is slightly extended the second time to prepare for a modulation to the dominant. Flourishes on the harp (the first ascending, leading into fig. 58; the second descending, just before fig. 59) add to the glittering character of the music.

Second subject: fig. 59–64

The second subject commences the moment the music cadences into C♯ minor on the downbeat of fig. 59. There is no mistaking the slightly grim march-like character that is due to a combination of factors:

➢ The insistent repeating crotchets at the start of the theme

➢ The detached staccato notes on the beat in the bass that alternate between C♯ and A (suggesting 'left, right, left' etc.)

➢ The dotted rhythms in bars 2 and 3 after fig. 59

> ➤ The slightly menacing rising sequence in bars 4–7 after fig. 59

> ➤ The dark tone of the violas and clarinets on the melody line (low flute and cor anglais are also used for the second bar to make a more snarling crescendo for the rising 5th)

> ➤ The dark tone of the low bassoons, horns and trombones in the accompaniment.

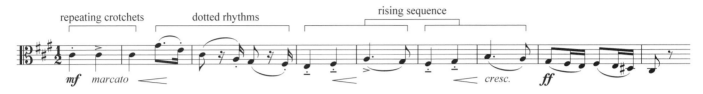

Further overlapping entries of the march theme occur: in a higher register (led by first violins) seven bars before fig. 60; and in the bass (including tuba) at fig. 60 a tone higher in D♯/E♭ minor. The texture becomes more animated (with flourishes in the flutes, for instance). At fig. 61 the theme is presented for the final time *fff* (including on all three trumpets) before the music reverts to the material of the transition.

The emotional temperature does not cool yet, and at fig. 63 there is an extraordinarily urgent tutti passage of descending overlapping triads at the top of the texture, which interlock rhythmically with rising 3rds in the bass line, each line following a circle of 5ths pattern:

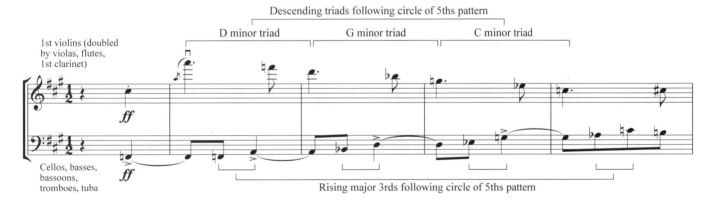

The momentum generated by this stormy passage at fig. 63 unleashes a furious 'con fuoco' return to the scherzo theme at fig. 64. With the exception of the double basses (which sustain a tonic pedal of F♯), all the strings play the theme *ff* (an electrifying effect with 50 players). The pedal note is also taken up by a long crescendo roll on the timpani, which leads to a crash from the cymbals, bass drum and snare drum.

Codetta: fig. 64–66

Near the start of the movement we saw Elgar deploy a touch of rhythmic augmentation to create the short phrase that leads into fig. 56. This phrase now returns at fig. 65 with further augmentation, not just from semiquavers into quavers but also into crotchets. This, coupled with a subtle chromatic shift that enables the music to reach a dominant 7th chord on F instead of a tonic chord on F♯, dissipates the energy and prepares the way for music of a very different character.

Exercise 17

1. Which percussion instruments play in the first bar of the movement?

2. What differences are there between bars 5–11 and the first eight bars of fig. 56?

3. What elements in the music make fig. 59 sound march-like?

4. What is the relationship between the tuba and the double bass at fig. 60?

5. What does the instruction 'IV' above the first violin stave after fig. 61 mean?

6. How does this instruction affect the sound?

7. What makes the music at fig. 64 sound so exciting?

8. What technique does Elgar use to alter the rhythm of the melodic line after fig. 65?

Trio section (in lieu of development): fig. 66–71

The trio has a largely ternary shape.

Trio opening section: fig. 66–68

The dominant 7th chord on F at the end of the codetta leads to B♭ major, which is the first use of major tonality in the movement. The music is altogether more delicate and naïve. Oboe and cor anglais sustain a ***pp*** inverted tonic pedal, while the flutes – intermittently supported by a solo violin (the leader of the orchestra) – present new thematic material. Essentially, it is a conjunct melody, apart from the frequent returning to its first note:

Apart from the tonic pedal, the accompaniment comprises some discreet contributions from divisi upper strings and a simple pattern on the harp. The latter oscillates between the tonic and the mediant (B♭ and D) in triplets. The alternation between these two pitches in a triplet rhythm forms a fascinating cross-rhythm. When recording the symphony in 1930, Elgar reputedly told his players to play this melody 'like something you hear by the river'. Listen carefully for this harp pattern: it seems to portray glimmering sunlight on the ripples of a river.

The trio theme is restated after fig. 67 and then extended by the strings as the music crescendos to fig. 68.

Trio middle section: fig. 68–70

With four bars of diminished 7th harmonies and a rapid descent through the strings, the temperature of the music becomes colder (like the sun going behind a cloud) and a new tune is heard in 3rds on the clarinets over a dominant pedal in G minor:

The new tune is taken up by the strings, before another four bars of diminished 7th harmonies provide a way out of this middle section that mirrors the way into it.

Trio final section: fig. 70–71

Flutes (assisted by some piccolo) and clarinets return to the B♭ major trio 'river' theme; the second violins take over the alternating B♭ and D that was heard previously on the harp at fig. 66 (now in semiquavers rather than triplets).

Just before the trio finishes, the theme from its middle section returns on the violins. This is then taken over by the winds at fig. 71 as the scherzo returns in the violas and cellos.

With its opening rising, conjunct pattern treated in falling sequence, this idea seems reminiscent of the sequential pattern of descending quavers that came in the earlier transition, which helps the overall cohesion of the movement.

Exercise 18

1. Describe Elgar's handling of texture at fig. 66.

2. What chord do the strings play on the *sf* downbeat of fig. 68?

3. Which of the instruments plays the lowest-sounding note at this point?

4. What differences in the musical texture are there between the first four bars of fig. 66 and the first four bars of fig. 70?

5. What key centres are used in the trio section (fig. 66–71)?

Recapitulation: fig. 71–77

This final section of the second movement follows the principles of a sonata rondo recapitulation: the second subject – the march theme – now appears for the first time in the tonic of F♯ minor at fig. 73. It has already been pointed out that the middle theme of the trio is still being played when the scherzo theme returns at fig. 71; in a similar contrapuntal way, the march and scherzo themes are heard juxtaposed at fig. 75.

Coda: fig. 77 to end of movement

With the standard sonata rondo plan nearing its close, Elgar includes a substantial coda. This final section comprises all of the movement's main ideas, as follows:

➢ Fig. 77: the key centre returns to B♭ major (and the imaginary riverbank) for a second substantial exploration of the trio material. Rather strikingly, it starts *ff*, almost as a parody, before relocating (after four bars) to the original delicate textures of its first appearance.

➢ Fig. 79: either side of this, we hear the theme of the middle of the trio, but now based in D minor rather than the previous version's G minor.

➤ Fig. 82: a return to F♯ minor and the scherzo theme; the trio's middle section theme is also present on violas and clarinets.

➤ Fig. 84: the scherzo theme is now skilfully manipulated with a fractional rhythmic augmentation – semiquavers now becoming triplet quavers. Chromatic alteration also changes the key to D♭ major at this point. A more straightforward rhythmic augmentation is also applied to the other scherzo melodic idea (originally heard two bars before fig. 56) as the music approaches fig. 85; quavers are now turned into crotchets.

➤ Fig. 85: the main trio theme is played again in B♭ major on flutes, clarinets and (at an upper octave) a solo violin.

➤ Fig. 86: the main scherzo theme is slowed further, now heard in quavers on second violins, violas and first harp, with a sense (though less secure this time) of D♭ major. Note that the movement's first melodic motif (i.e. bar 2 of the movement opening, on the low strings) is heard three bars before fig. 87.

➤ Fig. 87: there is further augmentation of the main scherzo theme. This is now heard on flutes and oboes in crotchets, while the low string motif twitches away in alternate bars. At fig. 88, the violins and violas play the crotchet version of the scherzo theme. Appearances of the twitching motif become more spaced out as the dynamic also reduces. Note how the tonic (F♯) is now becoming almost constantly present.

➤ Fig. 89: the scherzo theme is reduced to just its first four notes, the first of which is now extended to two-and-a-half bars in duration.

➤ Fig. 90: a very still, unwavering F♯ is now heard until (and beyond) the end of the movement. A few fragments of the march theme are heard at half speed, played so softly as to sound very distant.

Although the sense of F♯ minor lingers through the final bars of the movement, two significant notes are absent: G♯ and E♯. This helps Elgar to achieve his planned destination for the third movement: F♯, A, B, C♯ and D fit the keys of both F♯ minor and D major.

➤ Fig. 91: all the energy of the scherzo is now utterly spent, and there is a sense of something ethereal in the music. The bass line surrenders its low F♯ tonic four bars after fig. 91. Following a pizzicato reference to the march theme, the bass line has an occasional note – A or B – as though it is searching for something new.

Exercise 19

1. What key centre does Elgar use in his coda to the movement?

2. Identify the melodic themes that are heard at fig. 82.

3. What is rhythmic augmentation? In how many ways is the technique applied to the main scherzo theme in the coda?

4. In which instruments is an echo of the march theme heard at fig. 90?

5. At how many different octaves is a sustained F♯ heard at some point between fig. 90 and the end of the movement?

Third movement: Adagio

Overview

The second movement ends with the word 'attacca', which means to go on at once; there is no break at all between the two movements. In fact, Elgar guarantees this by making the final F♯ in the first violins and violas tie over the change of movements and become the first note of the Adagio. As the double bar at the end of the scherzo is crossed, the lone F♯ is joined by a richly scored string chord of D major. This is the new tonic for the third movement (and the destination of the wandering bass pizzicato notes played at the end of the scherzo).

This change of key happens at a *pp* dynamic, and creates a most tender and magical effect. More remarkable still is that the new melody initiated by the F♯ has exactly the same order of pitches as the scurrying and brittle scherzo theme. However, Elgar has changed the rhythm, tempo, articulation, harmonisation and texture, and the result is a musical world apart:

The joining of movements in this way was not the first time Elgar had used such a sleight of hand. In 1899 he had done something similar in the *Enigma Variations* at the start of the famous ninth variation 'Nimrod'. In both cases the tonic of one movement becomes the mediant of the next, and the first note of the new movement's melody.

In general, the structure of the Adagio follows the standard pattern of sonata form. The main sections are as follows:

Section	Figures	Comprising
Exposition	Bar 1 to fig. 98	First subject: from start to fig. 94
		Transition: fig. 94–96
		Second subject: fig. 96–98
Development	Fig. 98–100	
Recapitulation	Fig. 100–104	First subject: fig. 100–102
		Second subject: fig. 102–104
Coda	Fig. 104 to end of movement	

Exposition

The new version of the scherzo theme, with its slower pace and more intricate rhythms, makes for a beautiful string melody. What makes the opening to this movement so exquisite (other than

First subject: start to fig. 98

its magical arrival following the F♯ minor second movement) is Elgar's masterful handling of the texture. Through the texture, the strings carry the opening phrase of the Adagio; there is some very significant use of the winds to enrich the sound and blend in a touch of colour. Thus, in turn:

➤ The bass clarinet helps to give extra definition to the bass line in bar 1

➤ Two bassoons enrich the tenor register from bar 2, before handing over this role to two horns in bar 4

➤ Two clarinets in unison are used to give an extra bloom to the crotchet C♯ in the melody in bar 5

➤ The cor anglais reinforces the syncopation in the melody in bar 6

➤ Most but not all of the wind (no oboes) help to colour the peak of the phrase in the second half of bar 6

➤ The rich sound of a low flute is used to thicken the countermelody in bar 7, when the other winds have faded to *pp* and then silence.

Note that in this movement Elgar writes for 'Clarinets in A', which sound a minor 3rd lower than written.

Perhaps even more skilled is Elgar's scoring for the string section. The melody is scored with both depth and breadth: not only is the whole first-violin section playing the theme, but so too are the front desks of the second violins, violas and cellos. This spreads the sound of the melody around the front circle of the orchestra, and also adds to the rich violin tone the intensity of a high-register viola and cello timbre.

At fig. 93, freed from the connection with the scherzo theme, Elgar allows the Adagio melody to flow onwards into a second ravishing phrase. It starts with a memorably decorated fall of a minor 7th (A to low B via a tie, some triplet semiquavers and a dotted rhythm), and then climbs mostly stepwise through a 12th (compound perfect 5th) to an intense climax on a reiterated *ff* F♯. At this point the whole wind section and all four horns have joined the strings. In the middle of the luxurious texture the cor anglais, two bassoons, fourth horn, second violins and violas (minus front desks) play the scherzo theme once more. It is as though Elgar is drawing our attention to the thematic connection between the two movements in case we didn't notice it with the striking change of key and rhythm at the start of the Adagio.

A curious evaporation of the intensity through a contrary motion scale in the strings and on the bassoons links the end of the first subject to the transition.

Transition: fig. 94–96

The material of the transition involves some ornate melodic lines between fig. 94 and 95 in both the winds and the strings, while the texture is like a delicate web of interweaving lines. The harps are also significant here. In the two bars before fig. 95 a single falling melodic line in the winds has a constantly shifting scoring, often with a pair of instruments but always in unison:

➤ Flute and clarinet
➤ Flute and oboe

- Flute and bassoon
- Clarinet and bassoon
- Bassoon alone.

By contrast, the music from fig. 95 has a different character: quietly throbbing string chords reiterate in triplet anticipation of the beat and then tie onto the beat; mysterious, chromatic slow-moving crotchets alternate between two unusual instrument groupings:

- Two horns in octaves supported by low flute and low clarinet

- Cor anglais and bassoons.

Five bars before fig. 96 it seems that the music might be heading towards a minor key. Firstly E minor seems possible while there is a B in the bass, and then F♯ minor when the bass moves to C♯. In fact Elgar opts for a diminished 7th chord the bar before fig. 96 from which many options are possible. He chooses the brightness of A major, which is the standard dominant key for the second subject of an exposition.

The second subject is another tender and beautiful melody played by all the violins. Its opening involves wide leaps that seem to reach out longingly, and this idea is treated to a rising sequence. Meanwhile, a significant countermelody played by the violas in 3rds and clarinets in octaves, along with a solo cello, has a contrasting contour: it is conjunct and falling, reminiscent of the start of the motto theme. (However, the motto then had a rising 6th, which happens to be the interval of the main second-subject idea at this point):

Second subject: fig. 96–98

At fig. 97 Elgar inverts the texture: the main theme is in the tenor register, played by all the violas and cellos, while a decorated version of the countermelody is played by flutes, harps and violins. Note that the means of decoration echoes the flutes in the transition at fig. 94. The second subject then reverts to material from the transition, ending (rather inconclusively) at fig. 98.

Exercise 20

1. In what ways does Elgar use the scherzo theme in the first-subject area of the Adagio?

2. What do the following markings found in the first subject mean: cantabile, largamente, molto espress.?

3. Which transition theme is treated antiphonally between first and second violins?

4. What notes sound in the chord one bar before fig. 96?

Development: fig. 98–100

Elgar avoids an elaborate or intense sense of development in the middle of the movement. The slow tempo is not conducive to such workings, and in any case the result may have taken the emotional core of the movement away from the radiant first subject. Instead he concentrates on reworkings of his transition material. He does this by cutting the texture to an almost chamber-music scale, with a solo clarinet and solo violin to the fore playing florid melodic phrases.

Elgar's preparation for the return to D major at the recapitulation is significant. Instead of approaching it from the dominant (perhaps an A^7 chord), he brings the development to a close on the dominant 7th of F♯ minor, thereby underlining the movement's close relationship to the scherzo (which was, of course, in F♯ minor). He then resolves this chord, not as a perfect cadence but as an interrupted cadence. In a sense, this reminds us of the arrival into D major at the start of the movement.

Recapitulation: fig. 100–104

The first subject returns, though without any added colour from the winds (which perfectly complements the rich wind writing in the development). Listen out for the brief gesture on clarinets and bassoons four bars after fig. 100. Elgar also does without a transition this time. However, he finds a way to twist the tonal centre: remarkably, the second subject does not recapitulate in the tonic, but in the remote key of C♯ major at fig. 102.

Elgar keeps the second subject short this time; he finds a way back to D major, and adopts some transition material for a brief codetta at fig. 103. Just before fig. 104 the movement seems to be coming to a close, but Elgar has other ideas.

Coda: fig. 104 to end of movement

The coda to this movement is one of the great gems of Elgar's entire output: a passage of enormous beauty, poise and emotional reach, and at the end, peace. It is built around a new theme, which is centred on a yearning rising minor 7th – the shape being treated to a rising sequence:

The melody begins pp in the first violins. It builds in texture, sometimes through use of the theme (for example in the second violins after fig. 105); sometimes through various elaborate contributions, such as the clarinet before fig. 106; and sometimes even with reference back to transition ideas (clarinet three bars before fig. 107). In a long-reaching arch, it then subsides until the coda theme is heard one last time after fig. 107 played by muted strings. There are two features to listen out for at the close: the two short interjections of horn and muted trombones, which seem to look forward to an idea in the finale; and the soft radiance of the solo clarinet in the final cadence.

Exercise 21

1. What are the main key centres for the third movement?

2. How many different instrumental parts use mutes in the coda?

3. Referring to three different points within the third movement, illustrate the different ways in which Elgar writes for the clarinet.

4. Highlight the detail and skill with which Elgar writes for the string section in the Adagio.

Fourth movement: Lento – Allegro

Overview

Of the four movements, the finale is – structurally speaking – Elgar's most original construction. To help understand the movement, it is worth considering first the grandiose way in which it ends. The significance of the music heard from fig. 146 to the end brings the entire symphony full-circle. Elgar achieves this with a lavishly scored restatement of the motto theme – which was heard at the start of the symphony – and a version of the motto that is far more glorious and conclusive than the version at the end of the first movement at fig. 48.

Why is this significant? Firstly, this final passage reveals once and for all the true tonic of the symphony: A♭ major. The first movement began and ended in A♭ major, but its first subject in both the exposition and recapitulation was in D minor. The subsequent movements covered a scherzo in F♯ minor and an Adagio in D major: keys that relate more to D minor than A♭ major. Secondly, the nature of the motto theme is almost entirely diatonic. Deciding that the final destination of the symphony (and therefore this movement) was going to be a tonally-stable 2-minute passage of A♭ major, Elgar realised that there were some important priorities for the finale up until this point:

➤ Create a primarily restless movement

➤ Make the majority of the movement tonally unstable

➤ Avoid (largely) the key of A♭ major until the end.

To achieve this, Elgar devised the main body of the movement around a sonata-form shape, but one that does not follow the usual formula for key relationships: the first and second subjects appear in different keys in the exposition and the recapitulation to avoid giving a sense of a tonal home. Indeed, the key centres of these themes are not always easy to pin down: they do not start on a tonic (or even dominant) chord; they do not finish with key-defining cadences; and there are frequent chromatic inflections in melodic and harmonic aspects.

By understanding the relationship between tonal instability and the grand, tonally-stable coda in A♭, it becomes easier to locate the main sections of the movement, as follows:

Section	Figures	Comprising
Introduction (Lento)	Bar 1 to 5 bars after fig. 111	
Exposition (Allegro)	From 5 bars after fig. 111 to fig. 118	First subject: from 5 bars after fig. 111 to fig. 113
		Transition: fig. 113–114
		Second subject: fig. 114–116
		Codetta: fig. 116–118
Development	Fig. 118–134	
Recapitulation	Fig. 134 –141	First subject: fig. 134–136
		Transition: fig. 136–137
		Second subject: fig. 137–139
		Codetta: fig. 139–141
Coda	Fig. 141 to end of movement (after fig. 151)	

Introduction: start of the movement to five bars after fig. 111

It is not unusual for a sonata-form movement to start with a slow introduction. Here, however, it is not just a nod to convention; instead it fulfils a significant structural role, not just in the movement but in the symphony as a whole. In a relatively short passage Elgar incorporates several important features:

1. A reminder of D minor: after the third movement ends in D major, the finale begins by reminding us of the importance of the minor key of D that competed for supremacy in the first movement.

2. A direct link to the thematic material of the first movement: after the link between the second and third movements, Elgar returns to the angular theme first used at fig. 24 during the first movement's development.

3. The presentation of two important new themes: one that will be used as transition material; the other that will dominate the development section of the finale.

4. A reminder of the symphony's motto theme.

5. A brief glimpse of A♭ major, which will not return again until the coda. It is a reminder of the ultimate tonal goal. However, at this point, so close to the D minor introduction, it does not yet offer any sense of tonal stability. Had Elgar chosen to base the whole movement in A♭ major by building the sonata form on that key, the coda would not have such a sense of affirmation and homecoming.

Significant moments in the introduction, therefore, are:

➢ Bar 1: the ***ppp*** tremolando on D in the strings (supported by bass drum roll) to suggest mystery and darkness.

➢ Bar 2: the first movement's angular development theme from fig. 24 is played on the dark tones of the bass clarinet; the B♭ third note and the F♮ on the downbeat of bar 3 confirm the sense of D minor. The bassoon follows one bar later in canon.

➢ Bar 6: the first appearance of the theme that will dominate the finale's development is played staccato in a low register by bassoons and pizzicato cellos, creating a homophonic texture. With its falling conjunct crotchets in the first bar, this theme seems to connect with the start of the symphony's motto theme:

We have already had a glimpse of this theme – right at the end of the third movement Adagio, the muted horn and trombones hinted at it twice.

➢ Second bar of fig. 108: the first clarinet plays the first appearance of the theme that will be used in the transition:

➢ Third bar of fig. 108: the last desks of the first and second violins and viola (this instrumentation in itself is a reminder of the first movement) enter discreetly with the opening of the motto theme (overlapping in unison with the last note of the clarinet theme).

➢ Fig. 109: the introduction goes over much the same ground again, this time based on F rather than D, which is halfway between D and A♭.

➢ Fig. 110: A♭ major is reached; the angular theme is now treated to rhythmic diminution and played in quavers.

➢ Third bar of fig. 110: the motto theme is again played by the back desks, but this time in A♭ major – a clear hint of what to expect later on.

➢ Fig. 111: the chromatic twists of the transition theme destroy the fragile hint of A♭ major, and the introduction breaks off on a short ***sf*** dominant 7th chord of D minor.

Exposition: five bars after fig. 111 to fig. 118

First subject: five bars after fig. 111 to fig. 113

The first subject is dominated by insistent dotted rhythms. Perversely, the accompaniment provides rests when the melody plays notes, and notes when the melody is holding its dotted crotchets. The effect is one of huge drive and energy, reminiscent of fig. 63 in the scherzo, only much more prolonged. However, the lack of any conclusive use of the tonic makes this feel like music striving (but failing) to find a destination.

The dotted-crotchet-plus-quaver rhythm was used as part of the first movement themes (though not with the same intensity). Indeed, the first subjects of both outer movements share the same rhythm and contour in their respective fifth bars. There is little else to the first subject in the finale. As the music progresses, the texture expands and the dynamic increases.

Transition: fig. 113–114

The transition theme, stated in the introduction, is used three times in quick succession and in an approximate rising sequence. The triplet crotchets provide the perfect rhythmic foil to the first-subject material, and in the third phrase they follow a surging flourish in the upper strings. This is the climax and the music quickly subsides to *pp* one bar before fig. 114.

Second subject: fig. 114–116

The second subject is introduced by the clarinets, violas and cellos:

Although this theme sounds fresh in mood – being good-humoured and almost jaunty – it is constructed from familiar building blocks: the dotted rhythms of the first subject and the triplet crotchets of the transition theme. There is also a marching staccato bass line that reminds us of the bass line to the motto theme, and even an echo of the second subject of the first movement, with the octave leap followed by a falling 3rd.

Like the first subject, there is no confirmation of the key. However, despite the various chromatic inflections, there is a sense of B♭ major. The violins take up the second-subject theme at fig. 115.

Codetta: fig. 116–118

The codetta starts with the transition theme and then builds towards the start of the development with more driving rhythms. Similar patterns to the first subject are involved in the texture here, but there are also incisive syncopated entries on the clarinets and second violins, followed by flutes and violas. The harmony remains chromatic and the tonality is unstable.

Exercise 22

1. What thematic material is present in the introduction to the finale?

2. Which percussion instrument plays in the first four bars of the finale?

3. How does Elgar generate momentum in his first-subject material in this movement?

4. What rhythmic unit connects the transition theme and the second subject?

Development: fig. 118–134

The development of the finale is a lengthy passage, remarkable for its sustained restless energy. Elgar makes use of themes that are already urgent and tonally on the move to build a dynamic development, without any strong articulating cadences. This builds to a wondrous passage at fig. 130, which leads directly to the recapitulation.

Do not try to analyse the ever-shifting tonal scheme in this section. Instead, spot which themes are being used and marvel in Elgar's consummate handling of a large symphonic orchestra. Significant reference points in the development include the following aspects:

➤ Fig. 118: the development is announced by the appearance of the staccato theme from the introduction to the finale. Between fig. 118 and 120 there are five appearances that become increasingly assertive, rising in pitch and tonal centre, each successively more strongly orchestrated and louder. The entry four bars before fig. 120 has the whole orchestra hammering home the theme in a homophonic *ff* texture.

➤ Fig. 120: Elgar now turns his attention to the first-subject material – those driving dotted rhythms.

➤ Fig. 121: while the first-subject material drives on, the horns present a significant new figure that hones in on the triplet crotchets of the second subject.

➤ Fig. 122: the development now returns to the staccato theme based on conjunct crotchets. However, this time there are entries that invert into a rising pattern (for example, oboes and upper strings in the third bar of fig. 122).

➤ Fig. 124: the level of intense energy increases during this tumultuous passage, with angular thrusting strings and off-beat *sf* entries in the wind (doubled elsewhere in the strings).

➤ Fig. 125: further entries of the conjunct staccato theme – full wind answered by full strings – then more of the tumultuous material. Meanwhile, the triplet crotchet pattern appears in trumpets and then horns, followed by a simplified version on trombones.

➤ Fig. 126: the conjunct staccato theme now has overlapping entries on trumpets and horns.

➤ Fig. 127: Elgar now turns to his second subject, which is shared between various string and wind parts. Simultaneously, the energy level is kept high by various triplet patterns.

➤ Three bars before fig. 129: the music briefly halts unexpectedly on a first-inversion chord of A♭ minor, played *sf*; a familiar, detached marching bass line then takes the music forwards.

➤ Fig. 129: the motto theme is heard from the back desks of violins and violas (and clarinets), now in A♭ minor.

Fig. 130–134

This rhythmically augmented version of the theme highlights its connection to the motto theme, which we have just heard prior to this section: both themes start with a conjunct falling pattern.

After all the turmoil of the movement so far, with its constantly shifting tonal centres, chromaticism and driving rhythms, this final passage of the development stands out as an oasis of deep beauty and yearning. Elgar once more uses rhythmic augmentation (the technique that was so significant to the Adagio) and applies it to the conjunct staccato theme, also transforming staccato into a broad legato. This theme is now given a lush treatment, with overlapping contrapuntal entries that alternate between E♭ minor and its relative G♭ major. These broad cantabile lines are carried by the strings and upper wind over a glorious chordal accompaniment heard variously on bassoons, horns and trombones, while the harps add a glinting backdrop of arpeggios and spread chords.

Fig. 132 is one of the few places in the whole symphony where it is essential to have two harps in the orchestra.

With each successive entry of this yearning theme, the dynamic and orchestra builds. Listen out for how the trombones emphasise the downbeats from the ninth bar of fig. 132 in a slow throbbing rhythm. The final entry of the theme is dominated by all four horns in unison, sounding high in their range. The great wash of sound quickly breaks off at fig. 134 as the development ends.

Recapitulation: fig. 134–141

In most sonata-form movements, the recapitulation is the section of resolution, and the passage that balances the disruption of the development. That is not Elgar's plan here – he intends for his motto theme in the coda to be the resolution and fulfilment of the symphonic argument. Therefore, not only is this recapitulation a return to the tonally unstable driving rhythms of the first subject, but it begins in the very distant key of E♭ minor. However, as noted previously, the material never cements its tonal centre; neither starting from nor cadencing onto its tonic.

The return of the tonally unstable first subject perhaps explains why (unusually) the development culminates in the long passage of relatively stable E♭ minor/G♭ major. Its serenity throws light on the restlessness that returns in the recapitulation.

In due course, after the transition at fig. 136, the second subject is recapitulated at fig. 137 in G♭ major – the same relationship to the first-subject key as occurred in the exposition. The tonal resolution is still being withheld.

The codetta between fig. 139–141 follows the equivalent passage in the exposition (fig. 116–118).

Coda: fig. 141 to end of movement

The coda comes in two sections: a build in anticipation and then the return of the motto theme.

Elgar returns to the two themes that have already done so much work for him in this movement: the conjunct staccato development theme and the transition theme. The former launches the coda at fig. 141; the latter enters with weighty rhythmic augmentation on the horns at fig. 143, and then is altered in a different way to create the overlapping waves that are heard in the strings just after fig. 144.

At fig. 145 the trumpets have one of the longest of all anticipatory notes: eight bars of a held concert C (in octaves), which crescendos thrillingly from *mf* to *fff* in preparation to be the first note of the returning motto theme. In a far more excited way, many other leads across the texture here are anticipatory of the compound beats of this $\frac{6}{4}$ section. Listen out for the descending glissando on the two harps in the bar before fig. 146.

The motto theme returns for a full restatement. It is confident, tonally stable and resolving – not just of the energies of the last movement, but the symphony as a whole with all its thematic cross-references and unusual tonal relationships. The setting is the most scintillating passage of the whole symphony: the work of a true master of orchestration. Following many pages of heavy analysis, sit back and marvel at this awesome ending to the symphony.

The return of the motto theme: fig. 146 to end

Exercise 23

1. How does Elgar build intensity between fig. 118–120 at the start of the development?

2. Which instruments carry the main development theme (in its augmented version) between fig. 130–134?

3. Which instruments play the motto theme at fig. 146?

4. How much of the symphony is actually 'in A♭ major'?

5. Identify three different themes that appear in more than one movement of the symphony.

6. What passages are of special significance to the string players sat at the back desk of their section?

7. How significant is the technique of rhythmic augmentation in the symphony?

8. Choosing from two of the four movements, discuss two different passages that support the view that Elgar was a masterful orchestrator.

Shostakovich: Symphony No. 5

The composer

Dmitri Shostakovich (1906–1975) is a significant 20th-century composer; in the words of the *New Grove Dictionary of Music and Musicians* (Oxford University Press, 2001) he is 'regarded as the greatest symphonist of the mid-20th century'. He is also referred to as the voice of Soviet Russia; he expressed the experience of living under the oppression of communism (under the dictatorship of Joseph Stalin), while managing to avoid serious confrontation with that regime.

To us in 21st-century Britain, the thought of artistic suppression by a dictatorship seems foreign. However, the Russian communists took considerable interest in the work of artists; they would be quick to condemn any expression that was considered critical of the regime, or that included ideas from the 'decadent West'. For an artist, condemnation could easily and quickly lead to long-term imprisonment in a Siberian gulag (Soviet forced-labour camp), or even assassination. Ironically, it was working under this intense personal pressure that led Shostakovich to write his greatest

Stalin was General Secretary of the Communist Party from 1922 until his death in 1953. He was a fearsome leader: 'the measures taken by the dictator to 'discipline' those who opposed his will involved death by execution or famine of up to 10 million peasantry (1932–33)' (*Chambers Biographical Dictionary*, 1984).

music. No work better represents this than the music of his fifth symphony.

Shostakovich was born in St Petersburg, and only began piano lessons (with his mother) at the age of nine. He made rapid progress, however, and joined the Petrograd Conservatory in St Petersburg as a young teenager of 13 to study piano and composition. His graduation work (aged 19) was his Symphony No. 1. By 1928 it had been performed in America; meanwhile Shostakovich had written his second and third symphonies and his first opera *The Nose*.

In 1931 Shostakovich began work on a new opera: *Lady Macbeth of the Mtsensk District.* When it was first performed in 1934 (with twin premières in Leningrad – as St Petersburg had by now been renamed – and Moscow) the composer was very much under the spotlight. Initially, critical reception was favourable. However, this all changed in January 1936 when Stalin himself attended a performance; 11 days later, an article appeared in the communist party's newspaper *Pravda* ('Truth'). Entitled 'Muddle instead of music', the article was unsigned (the assumption was that it had been ordered by Stalin) and it castigated Shostakovich for his new work. Performance of the opera was soon banned.

Shostakovich was facing an extreme crisis. Overnight he had lost his place as the leading voice in Soviet music. Friends would not return his calls; people crossed the street to avoid him. He had already written his fourth symphony – his most challenging composition to date – and it was due for its first performance at the end of the year (1936). After many rehearsals, Shostakovich withdrew the piece; it is unclear under what pressure. His fourth symphony finally received its première in 1961, long after Stalin's death.

Somehow Shostakovich avoided arrest, and in 1937 took the remarkably courageous path of writing a new symphony: his fifth. The intensity of the première on 21 November 1937 was coupled with the stress of waiting for a verdict from those in authority. In the event the hall was packed; many people broke down and wept during the slow movement, and at the end the ovation lasted half an hour. With his new symphony, Shostakovich returned to being an approved artist.

After the death of Stalin in 1953, Russia entered a period now known as 'the thaw'. Shostakovich was able to travel and so visited the UK in 1958 and 1960. Nonetheless, life became harder again when Leonid Brezhnev came to power in 1964.

Shostakovich's last years were blighted by ill health, but he still composed. He died in 1975, long before the era of 'glasnost' (openness) and 'perestroika' (restructuring), which led to the end of the Soviet era. By then, Shostakovich had completed 15 symphonies; these, and the 15 string quartets he wrote, are the main pillars on which his reputation rests. He was enormously prolific in other areas too. Some of his works are considered inferior as they were written principally to placate the authorities; others, such as the first violin concerto and the late viola sonata, are wonderful works of enormous personal significance.

'Here is "Leftist" chaos instead of natural, human music. The power of good music to reach the masses has been surrendered to a petit-bourgeois "formalist" attempt to produce originality by means of cheap buffoonery. It is a game of ingenious trickery which may end very badly.' (*Pravda*, 28 January 1936)

The years 1937–1938 in Soviet history are known as 'the great terror'. It is estimated that seven million Russians were taken to the gulags (forced-labour camps) and in excess of half a million executed in just over a year. Some claim that even these figures are conservative.

'As the most talented Soviet composer of his cursed generation... his achievement is unrivalled.' (*The New Grove Dictionary of Music and Musicians*, Oxford University Press, 2001)

Symphony No. 5

Shostakovich wrote his fifth symphony in 1937. The work follows the standard four-movement symphonic pattern:

➢ First movement: Moderato

➢ Second movement: Allegretto (like a scherzo)

➢ Third movement: Largo

➢ Fourth movement: Allegro non troppo.

The reception of Shostakovich's fifth symphony in November 1937 was an important dual success. The authorities heard a more taut and economic musical language than the style that had been criticised in *Lady Macbeth*. Shostakovich had learned from his totalitarian reprimand; therefore, the symphony was not too complex in either technical or emotional content. The party considered that the music represented the journey of an intellectual from individualism to solidarity with the people – a journey that implicitly underlined the communist creed. In the climactic end to the symphony they heard the apotheosis of that communist creed. Aware of the political agenda, when it was suggested that the symphony was 'a Soviet artist's practical creative reply to just criticism', Shostakovich agreed.

The general public, however, who all shared the terror of the times, heard the music differently. In the slow movement, in particular, they heard a lament for the many who had 'disappeared' – a means of public grieving. Meanwhile, to the public, the finale was not the triumph of communism, but an expression of resilience.

It is difficult to know exactly what message Shostakovich intended to convey. However, in 1979 (four years after the composer's death), Russian musicologist Solomon Volkov (who had emigrated to the USA in 1976) published the book *Testimony*, which he claimed to be Shostakovich's memoirs. The authenticity of the book remains questionable, due to the fact that all the source material remained in Russia. However, in Volkov's book Shostakovich says of the finale of his fifth symphony:

> '... What exultation could there be? I think that it is clear to everyone what happens in the Fifth. The rejoicing is forced, created under a threat... It's as if someone were beating you with a stick and saying "Your business is rejoicing, your business is rejoicing", and you rise, shakily, and go marching off muttering "Our business is rejoicing, our business is rejoicing". What kind of apotheosis is that?'

In the 18th-century symphony (as in Beethoven's first) the slow movement is placed second. However, in the 19th century, it is more common for composers to put the slow movement third, at the 'heart' of the symphony; Beethoven's ninth symphony is a famous early example of this practice.

Scores: there are clear editions of the symphony in miniature score published by Eulenberg and Boosey & Hawkes. Shostakovich wrote numerical rehearsal marks into his score at regular intervals; these will be used to identify locations in the analysis that follows.

Recordings: the symphony has been recorded many times, and you will have no trouble finding a quality recording. For historical significance, you may want to listen to a performance conducted by Yevgeny Mravinsky, who was on the podium for the first performance. His final recording of the symphony was made in 1984 when the conductor was 81, with the Leningrad Symphony Orchestra. Of the more recent recordings, the one with the Royal Liverpool Philharmonic Orchestra conducted by Vasily Petrenko (on Naxos) is critically acclaimed. There are also several professionally filmed performances available on YouTube.

First movement: Moderato

Overview

The first movement of Shostakovich's fifth symphony is approximately 18 minutes long. It is based clearly on principles found in sonata form (though not without some innovative elements). The main sections are as follows:

Section	Figures	Comprising	Key
Exposition	Bar 1 up to fig. 17	First-subject area: start to fig. 9	Starts in D minor
		Second-subject area: fig. 9–17	Starts in E♭ minor
Development	Fig. 17–36		
Recapitulation	Fig. 36 to end of movement	First subject (subsidiary material only): fig. 36–39	Starts in D minor
			Starts in D major
		Second subject: fig. 39–44	Ends in D minor
		First subject: fig. 44 to end of movement (after fig. 47)	

Symphony No. 5 involves some fascinating twists compared to a more traditional version of sonata form. The following points are of particular interest:

➢ Compared to most examples of sonata form, the development section is disproportionately long: 124 bars, compared to 119 for the exposition and 73 for the recapitulation. This can be seen to reflect the context of turmoil and struggle that Shostakovich faced in 1937, and the lack of any clear resolution. (A substantial recapitulation would have brought a consolidating resolution to the movement.)

➢ The first-subject area is developmental, with several important motifs explored and manipulated in various ways. Its main melodic theme is heard at fig. 1; the preceding music therefore has the sense of being an integrated introduction.

➢ The second-subject area begins in the remote key of E♭ minor; just a semitone up from the tonic of D minor, it creates a very dark effect. Fig. 12–15 comprise some sense of development, starting in B minor. A restatement of the main second-subject material at fig. 15 could be seen as providing a codetta to the exposition.

➢ The return to a tonal centre of D minor at fig. 36 sounds more like the climax (and, to an extent, a continuation of) the development, rather than the recapitulation. Significantly, Shostakovich avoids returning to the opening material of the movement at this point, preferring instead to use subsidiary material (first heard after fig. 3).

➢ After the intense drama of returning to D minor at fig. 36, Shostakovich chooses to recapitulate the second subject starting in D major – even though it was not a major-mode theme in the exposition (fig. 39).

➤ The return of the main first-subject material at fig. 44 is still developmental (the main theme in inversion, for instance) and provides a coda to the movement.

Exposition: start to fig. 17

The opening four bars that lead to the main first subject are not just introductory, but are built from some significant motifs:

First-subject area: start to fig. 9

➤ The upward-thrusting double dotted figure in bar 1

➤ The three-note falling conjunct motif heard in sequence in bar 3

➤ The three repeated As in the violins in bar 4, which move onto a strong beat.

At the opening of the first movement the violins are in close canon, one beat apart, with the cellos and basses; they then move by contrary motion to meet on the significant As in bar 4, as shown in the following example:

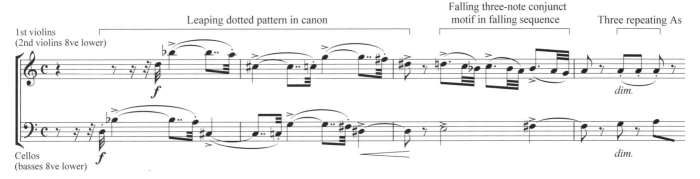

The opening dotted rhythms now calm down a little (no longer double dotted, and *p* rather than *f*) to create an accompaniment pattern that alternates between violas and cellos/double basses. With the absence of any 3rd to the harmony, the effect is cold and stark. At fig. 1 the first violins enter with a distinctly mournful theme. Not only is it slow and falling, including the F♮ of D minor, but the melody also has the dark E♭ of the Phrygian mode. (The C♮, or flattened seventh, on the downbeat of the third bar of the melody at fig. 1 is also from this mode.) By the sixth bar of the theme, Shostakovich has used all 12 tones of the chromatic scale; note that all visitors to the overall tonality of D minor have been ominous flats rather than brightening sharps, as shown in the example below.

Shostakovich's use of all 12 pitches in his theme is not akin to the 12-tone atonal music that serial composers such as Schoenberg had written around this time. Instead it is indicative of the Russian composer's sense of extended tonality in which all the chromatic notes can be used in a way that still points towards the tonic (D).

The theme at fig. 1 is not unrelated to the introductory bars – in its fourth and fifth bars it includes the same three-note falling conjunct motif that was presented in bar 3. (The first bar of the theme could be seen to relate to this in a rhythmically augmented manner.)

At fig. 2 the music of the opening bars is heard, now reworked a tone lower. There is a very dry timbre of bassoons, pizzicato cellos and double basses under tremolando violins. Note the rhythm of the repeating Es in the lower strings two bars before fig. 3, which is similar to the violins two bars before fig. 2.

At fig. 3 the first violin plays the three-note figure a perfect 5th higher, to decorate the opening of the main first-subject theme. The repeating As appear again. The melodic line that follows (either side of fig. 4, see the example below) seems rather innocuous. At this point it is supported by a light texture in the upper strings, but it will be of enormous significance in the recapitulation (fig. 36). The same melody is also heard in the cellos at fig. 6.

Much of what follows in the first-subject area is built from the elements introduced during the first four figures of the movement: the main first-subject theme; the three-note motif; the repeating-note rhythm that drives to a strong beat; the leaping dotted-rhythm idea. This all builds to a $\boldsymbol{f\!f}$ climax at fig. 7 in which all of these ideas are present. There is an intensification of the harmonic palette with a piquant chord setting F♯ against F♮ the bar before fig. 8 – the semitonal clash is known as a false relation.

After fig. 8 the strings return briefly to the opening canonic treatment of the leaping dotted rhythms, which then melts away on the horns and bassoon.

Second-subject area: fig. 9–17   There is a fascinating texture for the main second-subject idea: soft, throbbing chords that use the repeating note rhythms (long–short–short–long etc.), which link back to the repeating As in bar 4; the harp punctuates the chord changes; in the high register, the first violins play a strange melody that moves slowly by wide leaps, as follows:

It seems likely that the inspiration for this theme came from the famous Habanera from Act 1 Scene 5 of Bizet's *Carmen*:

Shostakovich has kept the same rhythm pattern (though notated as rhythmically augmented) and the repetitive rhythm of the thrumming accompaniment echoes the habanera pattern; he has also used a similar melodic contour, but with some of the intervals stretched. The harmonic rhythm through this passage is slow, and the chords that Shostakovich uses include some mild dissonances such as 7ths and various chromatic shifts. The whole effect is one of loneliness with nostalgic echoes haunting the air.

At fig. 12 the upper half of divisi violas continue with similar melodic material to the main second-subject theme; their desk partners and cellos engage in a simple dialogue using the rhythm of the three-repeated-notes figure – but now with a pitch set that starts with a gloomy minor 3rd each time.

An interlude commences at fig. 13. Richly scored (the contrabassoon is significant here), repeating chords are answered by a solo flute that picks up on the minor 3rd pattern of the preceding viola and cello accompaniment. After a brief surge from strings and winds, the interlude is brought to a close by an unaccompanied clarinet solo.

At fig. 15 the main second-subject theme returns, scored in a similar way to fig. 9 but with the tune on the yearning sound of the violas. The passage begins in B minor, but soon returns towards Eb minor. The violas revert to the minor 3rd figure used in the accompaniment at fig. 12; this figure then passes downwards to the cellos as the exposition ends.

Why did Shostakovich use Bizet's tune as a source for this theme? The lyric gives a clue. In 1934–35 Shostakovich had been in love with a translator called Elena Konstantinovskaya. However, after a short time in prison, she married the filmmaker Roman Karmen. It would seem that, even at the height of political pressure, Shostakovich was finding a chance to add a personal element to his symphony.

Exercise 24

1. What similarities and differences are there between the first two bars of the symphony and the second and third bars of fig. 2?

2. What are the four significant melodic ideas presented in the music up to fig. 3?

3. What common element is there between the music four bars after fig. 3 and two bars after fig. 6?

4. What differences are there between the first two bars of the symphony and the second and third bars after fig. 8?

5. In what ways does Shostakovich take care with articulation between fig. 9–12?

6. How is the melodic interval of a minor 3rd (in quavers) significant between fig. 12–17?

Development: fig. 17–36

The development can be viewed as a number of composite sections, which create a steady accumulation of energy and intensity.

There is an immediate new intent as the development starts on the final beat of the bar at fig. 17, not least due to the dynamic change to *f* (from *pp* a bar earlier). An insistent ostinato-like bass line is launched by the piano, with pizzicato cellos and double basses. The ostinato is based on the minor 3rd pattern heard at fig. 12. However, some of the intervals are now reduced to a menacing diminished 3rd (e.g. E to Gb). The ostinato also creates a persistent rhythmic pattern of two quavers plus a crotchet, which was first (seemingly innocently) presented in the fourth bar of the symphony, and given more importance at fig. 8.

First section: fig. 17–19

Layered onto this ostinato, though very much in the same bass register, is the main first-subject theme played on all four horns:

1st subject in exposition at fig. 1 (1st violins)

1st subject in development at fig. 17 (horns at sounding pitch)

Fig. 17 is the first appearance of the piano in this symphony. The piano was virtually unknown in the orchestra before the 20th century, apart from as a solo instrument for a concerto. In Symphony No. 5 Shostakovich draws on the piano's brittle, percussive quality; its low notes have a more penetrating clarity than low pizzicato strings. An interesting work to compare this to is the *Symphonic Dances* by Rachmaninov – another Russian composer, but one who had gone into exile in the west when the communists came to power in Russia.

Shostakovich's orchestral writing often explores extremes of register. In fig. 17–18, he finds a very black tone quality from the low horns, perhaps to convey the sense of terror that the composer knew all too well.

At fig. 19, listen out for the strident colour of the small E♭ clarinet in the blend of woodwind; the instrument adds significantly to the vibrancy of the sound.

Note that when the horns play in the bass clef, the transposition to sounding pitch is up a perfect 4th rather than down a perfect 5th. The theme is treated to various rhythmic augmentations. At fig. 18 the trumpets enter with similar material, creating an increasingly contrapuntal texture. Note the 'poco animando' (a little animated) indication.

Second section: fig. 19–22

As the ostinato line climbs out of the low register (basses are no longer involved, for example), the tempo increases to ♩ = 104. The upper woodwinds have an entry of the main first-subject theme, now in its original note values, but with an altered pattern of tones and semitones. This grows into a longer phrase through the use of a scurrying upwards scale, a bar of dotted rhythms (reminiscent of the opening to the symphony), and a bar that refers back to the motif first heard in bar 3.

The melodic material propels the music forward for a while, with the violins also becoming involved. Listen out for the snarl on the horns at fig. 21, now very much at the top of their register, as seen in the following example:

Horns before fig. 21 (sounding pitch)

Third section: fig. 22–25

The tempo increases again to ♩ = 126. The music gains extra momentum from the staccato quaver pattern in the trumpets, which is based on the significant minor 3rd interval that was established at fig. 12. At fig. 22, Shostakovich now includes the second-subject melody in the development process, firstly on the low strings and then, a bar later, in the winds. The melody is treated to rhythmic diminution and played *ff* with accents; as a theme that first appeared poignant and deeply personal, it now sounds brutal, as seen in the comparison below:

1st violins at fig. 9 (exposition):

Cellos and basses at fig. 22 (development):

In the third bar of fig. 22 the three-note falling conjunct motif appears sequentially, first in the winds and then more extensively in the strings. This now creates a driving rhythm based on a pattern of two semiquavers plus a quaver – a diminution of the two quavers plus a crotchet pattern already met. It links this material not only to the falling motif, but also rhythmically to the repeating-note figure of bar 4. At fig. 24 the trumpets reinforce the link by playing this rhythmic pattern to repeating notes. The dotted rhythms from the opening of the symphony return in the bass after fig. 23, and there are further references to the second subject at fig. 24 in canon between bass and treble.

Once more, Shostakovich increases the tempo ($\downarrow$ = 132). Beginning at fig. 25, the relentless momentum is continued with the motor rhythms passing from upper strings to trumpets and back again. For a couple of bars there are leaping minor 6ths in the horns and low strings, which link back to the start of the symphony. Further entries of the main first subject are then heard in canon between wind and low strings.

Fourth section: fig. 25–27

After fig. 26 the wind section joins the violins with the two semiquavers + quaver pattern, and the texture begins to fill out with the addition of the brass. The combination of crescendo and poco stringendo creates a sense of the music surging towards fig. 27.

A dynamic entry of the percussion marks a strong change of mood, as a grotesque parody of a march erupts on the trumpets. There are various martial trappings:

Fifth section: fig. 27–29

➢ The 'left-right' effect of alternating bass notes on the timpani, tuba and pizzicato double basses, a perfect 4th apart (suggestive of tonic-dominant)

➢ The motor rhythm now played incessantly on the snare drum

➢ The dotted rhythms in the trumpet melody from the third bar of fig. 27.

Despite these features, however, the march tune at fig. 27 starts with a variant of the first-subject main theme; it has been subverted from being a haunting, mournful theme into an ostentatious, militaristic anthem. Part of the transformation is from the original version of the theme in the dark Phrygian mode (with its flattened second), to the appearance of the theme in the brightest of the modes, the Lydian (with a sharpened fourth).

1st violins at fig. 1 (exposition):

Phrygian scale based on D

p

1st trumpet at fig. 27 (development):

Lydian scale based on F

ff

Sixth section: fig. 29–32

There are various ideas about why Shostakovich becomes fixated on the note A in this symphony (most notably at the end of the finale). The conductor Kenneth Woods writes that the composer once explained that 'La' was his nickname for Elena Konstantinovskaya, and 'La' is the note A in the tonic sol-fa system used in Russia to name notes. Woods also recounts that Shostakovich told another friend it represented the Russian word 'Ya' ('Я') meaning 'I' or 'me'. This raises unanswerable questions about the personal or political agenda to this music, but we certainly hear great intensity building here.

After fig. 28 Shostakovich adds various wind instruments to the parade, carefully selecting tone colours that will add to the shrill quality of the music: piccolo, high flute and oboe, and the small E♭ clarinet.

The marching F–C timpani continues for two more bars with a frenzy of activity above. The momentum is then carried forward by a long string of As played by the brittle xylophone, with wind and violins in support, playing the now familiar two semiquavers plus a quaver pattern. In all, there are eight bars of this persistent A rhythm.

Under this persistent motor rhythm on the note A, the bass instruments of the orchestra (led by the trombones) blast out a rhythmically augmented version of the opening dotted rhythms in canon. Then, as this continues at fig. 30, the trumpets and horns add the main first-subject theme to the ferocious melee. As the timpani and snare drum re-enter, the whole texture descends with dissonant chords, while another poco stringendo gives the music a sense of a headlong descent into terror.

Seventh section: fig. 32–36

It is at fig. 32 that the tempo reaches its fastest speed: ♩ = 138. The wind and strings engage in a furious version of the movement's opening dotted rhythms played *ff*. Meanwhile the second subject is transformed into a tyrannically monstrous melody, played *ff* by trombones and tuba, and then in canon by the horns (and from fig. 34 the trumpets).

Four bars after fig. 35, the trombones drop out and there is an intense build-up on A with the dotted-rhythm figure (note the two octave leaps in the cellos). There is a sense of a hole in the bass waiting to be filled, almost like the sea retreating before a tsunami is about to hit.

Exercise 25

1. What is the thematic origin of the material used at the start of the development (fig. 17)?

2. In the fourth bar of fig. 22, how many instruments are playing (sounding) A♭ in crotchets?

3. Where does Shostakovich make use of canon during the development section?

4. Which themes are treated in rhythmic augmentation or diminution?

5. Give three examples of Shostakovich using extreme registers of pitch in his orchestration during the development section.

6. The development can be seen as one long process of intensification. How does Shostakovich achieve this effect?

Recapitulation: fig. 36 to end of movement

With the space created in the bass register four bars after fig. 35, the anticipation builds. At fig. 36 (now marked ♩ = 66), the full orchestra sounds a deafening chord of a bare 5th on D, played *fff*. The timpani prefaces it with a semiquaver anacrusis, and a cymbal crash provides an extra element of thrill. This mighty D would seem to mark a traditional recapitulation, with the return of the tonic tonality. We are, however, a world away from the start of the movement, and Shostakovich refrains from using the main first-subject material. Instead, in a remarkable passage, he uses the subsidiary material from either side of fig. 4. From this he creates a melodic line that is played by all winds except bassoons, all four horns, and all strings (except basses) spread over four octaves. Only occasionally is the D chord resounded by the heavy brass and timpani, and never with its 3rd.

As the intensity of this passage fades after fig. 38, the opening dotted pattern appears once more in the bass instruments: bassoon, trombone, tuba, cello and double bass. Above is the repeating-note figure, once more on A, and now back as two quavers plus a crotchet.

The fury has passed; in a few bars the music slows, and reduces to *pp*. At fig. 39 (now ♩ = 84) the second subject returns in its original soft, floating guise and – for a while, at least – in the peaceful context of D major. After fig. 41 the tonality returns to more minor modes.

From fig. 42, Shostakovich writes a passage similar to that from the exposition at fig. 12, now rescored for oboe, clarinet and bassoon. At fig. 43 the horns play chords similar to those heard on clarinets and bassoons at fig. 13, and the cellos play an abbreviated version of the tune that was a flute solo in the exposition.

Only now does Shostakovich return to the main first-subject theme. However, he does so in an enigmatic fashion, treating it to inversion, while maintaining its cold Phrygian colour. In fact, this passage sounds more like a coda: the movement ends sombrely with lonely solos on the piccolo and first violin, an echo of the opening leaping dotted-rhythm shape in the cellos and basses, and eerie chromatic scales on the celesta.

First subject (subsidiary material only): fig. 36–39

Interpreting the meaning of this symphony is far from straightforward. Some, led by Ian MacDonald in *The New Shostakovich* (Pimlico, 2006), claim that this passage represents the dictator silencing all critics; others, for example Richard Taruskin in *Shostakovich Studies* (Cambridge University Press, 1995), prefer the view that the unison passages 'represent the efforts of the brutalised subject... to regain a sense of control at any cost'. Undoubtedly, the music represents struggle; in the end the listener must make their own sense of it. It is the mix of the clear powerful expression of the music, coupled with the ambiguity of specific meaning, that make this a great symphony – and one that satisfied both the party machine and the Russian people in 1937.

Second subject: fig. 39–44

First subject: fig. 44 to end of movement (after fig. 47)

Exercise 26

1. How does the melody between fig. 36 and fig. 38 relate to material in the exposition?

2. What differences are there in the treatment of the second subject at fig. 39 compared to its original appearance at fig. 9?

3. After the tranquillity of D major at fig. 39, how does Shostakovich create a more unsettled feeling before the end of the opening movement?

4. Which instruments play the bass line of the texture from fig. 47 to the end?

5. Which instrument doubles the trumpet part in the final four bars?

Second movement: Allegretto

Preliminary matters

In the Classical period, the second movement of a symphony was usually the slow movement, with a minuet and trio coming third. During the 19th century some changes to this pattern occurred. Firstly, largely due to Beethoven, the minuet gave way to a scherzo and trio – a more lively and glittering piece. Some composers, such as Beethoven and Brahms, wrote quite ferocious scherzos with strong driving rhythms, while others such as Mendelssohn and Tchaikovsky made their scherzos rather lighter with some deft and delicate orchestration. Secondly, during the 19th century it became more usual to have the scherzo as the second movement and delay the slow movement to be the third in the symphony, at the heart of the work. Beethoven's ninth symphony was an influential example of this new order.

Overview

Traditionally a scherzo and trio consists of a ternary form, with the scherzo section played again as a da capo after the trio. As a forerunner of the minuet, each section may use binary form, as shown in the following table:

Scherzo		Trio		Scherzo	
A	B	A	B	A	B
repeated	repeated	repeated	repeated	not repeated	not repeated

The second movement of Shostakovich's Symphony No. 5 clearly follows many of the characteristics and patterns of a scherzo and trio. However, to add more interest, the composer reworks the scherzo section after the trio, rather than relying on a simple da capo.

The movement uses the key of A minor as its tonal centre, with the trio in the relative key of C major.

The main sections are as follows:

Section	Figures	Comprising
Scherzo	Bar 1 to fig. 57	Introduction: up to fig. 49 A section: fig. 49–53 B section (first time): fig. 53–55 B section (second time): fig. 55–57
Trio	Fig. 57–65	A section (first time): fig. 57–59 A section (second time): fig. 59–61 B section (first time): fig. 61–63 B section (second time): fig. 63–65
Scherzo	Fig. 65 to end of movement (after fig. 74)	Introduction: fig. 65–66 A section: fig. 66–69 B section (first time): fig. 69–71 B section (secomd time): fig. 71 to three bars after fig. 73 Codetta: three bars after fig. 73 to end of movement

After the complexities of the opening movement, the second movement is rather more straightforward.

Scherzo: start to fig. 57

The tonal sense is A minor, but in a modal way. Shostakovich avoids the leading note of G♯ and instead uses B♭ to create a Phrygian character (the mode referred to in the first movement). The introduction comprises a solitary bass line played by cellos and basses. Its mix of crotchets and quavers creates a sprightly energy. There are some significant repeating As in bar 5: this is not just the tonic note for the first time, but related to melodic material that is going to appear later on in the movement (for instance at fig. 52).

Introduction: bar 1 up to fig. 49

The opening phrase starts on five woodwinds and forms a powerful unison in a high register; within three bars, the passage becomes a solo for the E♭ clarinet. The example below shows how trills, staccato notes and some unexpected angular leaps (just when it had seemed set to be a conjunct melody) make for a playful character. The only accompaniment comes from light staccato chords from the horns on beats 1 and 2, which creates a clear dance feel.

A section: fig. 49–53

E♭ clarinet (sounding pitch)

From fig. 50 there is some homophonic writing for the wind section. The bassoon has the most important line here, which soon becomes the solo melodic line, accompanied by just the cellos and basses. Note how from fig. 51 the low strings have the same bass line as they had in the introduction.

The violins – seconds followed by first – soon take over from the bassoon. Their melodic material is largely repeating quavers and short scalic patterns. Four bars before fig. 53, the lower strings drop out and leave the violins playing a pattern of falling broken chords. This pattern in the violins is combined with accents that create a playful hemiola feel.

The linking passage in the violins ends on G at fig. 53; Shostakovich uses this as a means of starting the B section in the key of C minor. A new melodic phrase appears at fig. 53 in all the woodwind except bassoons. Formed essentially from staccato dotted-rhythm patterns, the melody skips along attractively until three bars before fig. 54, where it reverts to the shape found in bar 2 of the A phrase. The accompaniment here is provided by percussion, trombones and strings and – but for the surprise of a ⁴₄ bar – is the pastiche 'oom-pah-pah' pattern of a waltz.

B section (first time): fig. 53–55

At fig. 54 the horns play a new melody in a two-part texture, which is based in F major. Timpani, bassoons and low strings play heavily in the bass on beats 1 and 2 of each bar; this creates a more parodied sense of a dance. The second phrase of the melody incorporates a rising scale (three bars before fig. 55). At this point, a playful violin line includes glissandos and a cross-rhythm.

B section (second time): fig. 55–57

This section is, essentially, the same as the previous section and represents one of the repeats in a traditional scherzo (see the table on page 64). There are some changes of orchestration to identify: the staccato, dotted-rhythm melody is now in the strings, instead of the woodwind.

Trio: fig. 57–65

A section (first time): fig. 57–59

Trios are often lighter in texture and scoring than the minuet or scherzo that precedes them. This is certainly the case here, as Shostakovich gives the melody to the leader of the orchestra who is only accompanied by simple harp chords and pizzicato cellos, which play broken chords in crotchets. Although the melody – aided by its C major setting – sounds new, it has several elements already presented in the scherzo. These include repeating staccato quavers, glissandos and scale patterns, as shown in the following example:

There is also a sense of periodic phrasing here; coupled with the simple tonic-dominant harmony, this creates quite a Classical feel to the start of the trio. However, from fig. 58 there are various chromatic twists to the harmony and alterations to the tempo, which create a more coquettish character.

A section (second time): fig. 59–61

This section is a re-orchestrated repeat: a solo flute replaces the violin on the melody; the bassoons take over the cellos' role from the previous scoring. Listen out for the glissandos on not just the harp, but also the violas and cellos at fig. 60.

B section (first time): fig. 61–63

The strings play an unaccompanied melodic phrase in unison, spread across four octaves, which is constructed from two falling sequences, firstly of a two-bar phrase and then of a single bar. This starts clearly in C major, however chromaticism – for example, the horns entering on (sounding) F♯ – take the music briefly through some distant keys: D♯ minor two bars before fig. 62, and then B major when low flute, oboes and clarinet enter with the theme that opens the trio. The *ff* entry before fig. 63 quickly re-establishes C major.

B section (second time): fig. 63–65

As with the first half of the trio, this section is a rescored repeat of B. The wind section (replacing the strings) takes the first phrase, which is slightly decorated (though Shostakovich does not expect the bassoonists to play the demisemiquaver scales!).

Scherzo: fig. 65 to end of movement (after fig. 74)

Much of this section follows the same path as at the start of the movement. You will be able to see and hear various alterations in the orchestration. In particular, listen out for the change to C♯ minor instead of C minor for the start of the B section at fig. 69 (equivalent to fig. 53); its repeat (at fig. 71) reverts to C minor.

The short codetta is based on the trio material. It starts with a mournful solo oboe, which makes the rising intervals smaller than when originally heard at fig. 57. The final flourish at fig. 74 has a touch of canon (two beats apart) between the top line and the bass.

Exercise 27

1. What elements make this movement point towards the character of a scherzo?

2. What tonal centres are used during the course of the movement?

3. How does Shostakovich give this movement a sense of a dance?

4. In what ways does the trio contrast with the outer sections of the scherzo?

5. How does the beginning of the codetta differ to the start of the trio?

Third movement: Largo

Overview

There is no mistaking the aura of grief conveyed by the symphony's slow movement. Written in F♯ minor, it was possibly composed in response to the execution by Stalin's forces of Shostakovich's friend and patron Marshal Tukhachevsky. During the 1930s, all Leningrad citizens would have had friends and family members who had recently been shot or had 'disappeared'.

In a memoir written in 1989 (*Story of a Friendship*, Faber 2001), Leningrad citizen and theatre historian Isaak Glikman wrote of the first performance of the symphony, 'I was very shaken to see that during the Largo... many, very many were weeping: both women and men.'

The orchestration for the movement is of immediate interest. Shostakovich does not use the brass section (including horns) at all. Most of the material is carried by the strings, which he subdivides into eight parts instead of the normal five: three separate violin parts, two viola parts and two cello parts, as well as the double basses. This creates a rich and expressive texture. The harp is also significant.

The woodwind instruments are mainly used as lonely solo voices (flute, oboe and clarinet) against tremolo strings. Then at the searing climax (fig. 89) strings and woodwind combine forces with the xylophone to an intense effect. There are also some touches of colour from the glockenspiel (just before fig. 87) and celesta (fig. 96).

This great elegiac movement took the composer just three days to write. It follows no standard form, but a number of musical paragraphs can be heard as the emotional power of the music grows and, finally, subsides. There are four main sections, which we can represent with the letters A to D as follows.

A slow-moving, wistful melody is heard on the third violins. It is set in a plaintive three-part string texture, in which the first violas play a countermelody that starts in 6ths with the violins

Fig. 75 (start): idea A

but soon finds a more astringent affect. There are two significant motifs early on in the violin melody: the repeating As in bars 2–3, which are decorated by a single fragile step up to B; and the sequential figure in bars 3–5 that harks back to the third bar of the first movement:

From bar 7 the melody reaches out with some upwards leaps, which start to convey some sense of loss. The falling-sequence motif occurs in the bass two bars before fig. 77. Three further lines of strings join at fig. 77 to enrich the texture. Doleful, falling chromatic-scale patterns become significant, and there are plangent dissonances in the harmony.

Fig. 78: idea B The entry of the first violins marks the second idea. It starts strikingly with three repeated marcato crotchets, which link to the falling-sequence motif; this motif of two bars is then repeated a minor 3rd higher with greater intensity:

The melodic line then transfers to the first cellos. During this idea, the other string lines play sustained chords to support.

Fig. 79: idea C The rich string texture yields to a solitary high flute and a gentle harp accompaniment. The opening bar of the flute melody is reminiscent of the main first-subject theme from the first movement. This impression is reinforced by the entry of the second flute playing an inversion of the same melody at fig. 80. A meandering cello line in quavers takes over from the harp towards the end of the passage.

Fig. 81: return of idea A A second exploration of idea A starts in B minor at fig. 81; it soon becomes more intense than at the start of the movement. This is achieved through dynamics and orchestration. Shostakovich blends the woodwinds into the string writing, and at the Largamente after fig. 82 there is a *ff* climax built around the dotted-rhythm chromatic-scales material.

Fig. 83: brief return of idea B In the aftermath of the climax at the Largamente, the cellos and double basses provide a reminder of idea B at fig. 83, with its initial repeating crotchets played in a bare manner without any accompaniment. The first violins enter with a similar meandering line of quavers to that played by the cellos before fig. 81, now played tremolo. This string technique is an important colour in the music from this point on. One might interpret it as portraying a chill, or a frightened nervousness.

Fig. 84: idea D The central, extended section of the movement is built around three woodwind solos for oboe, clarinet and flute respectively; each solo is supported by a fragile tremolo note played by one of the three violin sections. The three melodies start with the same motif, and shapes from the movement's other ideas appear in places – especially two bars of idea A at fig. 86, played in C♯ minor. The music through this passage is very forlorn.

At first this sounds like a recapitulation, with the opening string idea now played by clarinets and bassoons, back in the movement's tonic key of F♯ minor. However before long, the music begins its inexorable rise to what is going to be the most emotionally laden climax of the whole symphony. The build up of intensity is achieved by the following means:

Fig. 87: return of idea A

➢ Dynamics

➢ Increasing contrapuntal complexity

➢ Harmonic dissonance

➢ Use of cellos in a high register

➢ Chord changes accenting the weaker beats of the bar (before fig. 89).

With the intensity sustained by tremolo violas and second violins, combined with support from the piano, the full power of the repeating crotchets from idea B is unleashed *ff* and accented. The entry of the xylophone is particularly telling, and the E♭ clarinet also reinforces this savage moment. The rising scale played by bass instruments (two bassoons, contrabassoon, cellos and double basses) is also menacing and doom-laden.

Fig. 89: the movement's climax, using idea B

There is little weakening of the emotional temperature here as tremolo continues in various string parts and is reinforced by low clarinets. The cellos in a high register play idea D (now *ff*). Other motifs occur such as the repeating crotchets from idea B three bars before fig. 91, which then links into a shape first found two bars before fig. 85. Two bars after fig. 91, idea A returns on the violins (all three divisions now played in unison); this forms a counterpoint to the continuing cello melody (which is now doubled by flute, oboe and E♭ clarinet).

Fig. 90: return of idea D, with other motifs

The intensity finally abates; the A section is heard *pp* with muted strings. The first violins play a deadly slow rising chromatic scale, as the compass of the string texture widens to cover more than five octaves.

Fig. 93: the last appearance of idea A

Three of the movement's four main ideas were involved at the height of the climax. Idea C, which was the only one that escaped a vehement transformation, now returns with its harp accompaniment. The melody is heard here on the second violins instead of a woodwind solo. Meandering quavers return on the cellos and basses after fig. 95.

Fig. 94: return of idea C

Under a *pp* tremolo F♯, played high on the first violins, idea D is played as harmonics on the harp and doubled on the celesta. The effect is like ice: beautiful and pure, yet cold and desolate. A final string chord on F♯ major – in effect, a tierce de Picardie – offers little consolation after the emotion wrought by the movement.

Fig. 96: idea D closes the movement

Exercise 28

1. In what ways does Shostakovich configure his orchestra differently for the third movement?

2. How do the melodic ideas of the Largo connect with melodies found in the first movement?

3. What factors contribute towards the intensity of the movement's main climax?

4. What does 'con sord.' denote at fig. 93?

5. What playing technique is used on the harp after fig. 96?

Fourth movement: Allegro non troppo

Overview

For the finale, Shostakovich returns to the home key of the symphony – D minor – to maintain minor tonalities for all four movements (D, A, F♯ and back to D, respectively). However, the symphony turns from tonic minor to tonic major at fig. 131. There are famous precedents for this: Beethoven, Tchaikovsky and Mahler had each written fifth symphonies that began in a minor key and ended triumphantly and emphatically in a major key.

The question remains: what does the end of this symphony convey? Is it a triumphant hymn to the Soviet state? Or is it a defiant solidarity with the Russian people, in the face of terrible brutality and suffering? Then again, could it be the resilience of an artistic genius finding a way through the labyrinth of political persecution in order to create a symphony of authentic personal testament?

As in the Largo, Shostakovich largely avoids standard formal structures in the fourth movement; indeed Hugh Ottaway describes it as 'a brilliant improvisation, spontaneous but well directed' (*Shostakovich Symphonies*, BBC Music Guides, 1978). There is, however, a basic tripartite shape that just hints a little at some leftover vestiges of sonata form:

➤ First section (fig. 97–111): two themes stand out in this section. First is the opening march idea in D minor; second is the exuberant disjunct melody at fig. 110, which is clearly in A major – a dominant relationship that would be customary in an exposition.

➤ Second section (fig. 111–121): there is some thematic transformation of both the main themes presented in the first section, in the manner of a development. However, much of the passage is concerned with other material and is largely based in B♭, more like the middle section of a ternary structure.

➤ Third section (fig. 121–134): a lengthy dominant pedal on the timpani underpins the return to D minor and the start of a long build-up. This distant start to the section is atypical of a recapitulation, although the musical material is taken from the first section. Little use is made of the quasi second subject in the third section. When the climax finally reaches its D major destination, Shostakovich uses the march theme rather than the exuberant disjunct melody, which was the culmination of the first section.

Significant in understanding this movement is the link with a song called 'Rebirth' (*Vozrozhdeniye*, Op. 46 No. 1), which Shostakovich had written just before starting on the symphony. It is a setting of a poem by the Russian poet Alexander Pushkin.

The text of the song 'Rebirth' translates as follows:

An artist-barbarian with his lazy brush

Blackens the painting of a genius

And senselessly he covers it with

His own illegitimate drawing.

But with the passing years, the alien colours

Fall off like threadbare scales;

The creation of the genius emerges

before us in its former beauty

Thus vanish the illusions

From my tormented soul

And in it appear visions

Of original and innocent times.

It is possible to interpret that Shostakovich saw the barbarian artist in the poem as Stalin, who had 'blackened the paintings of genius', namely *Lady Macbeth of the Mtsensk District* and his fourth symphony. Richard Taruskin (in his essay in *Shostakovich Studies*) points out how the poet talks of an escape into the past, rather than a bright future. When, at fig. 120, Shostakovich quotes the accompaniment pattern from his song setting in the first violins, there is a sense of trying to hide in a half-forgotten dreamworld. Taruskin describes the return of the march theme after fig. 121 as a 'puncture... [a] sudden encroachment (of the present, of unsettling objective reality) on that subjective escape into the past'.

There is one further link between the song and symphony. The first four notes of the song, corresponding to 'An artist-barbarian', are A, D, E and F. These are used again as the starting notes for the main march theme of the finale to Shostakovich's fifth symphony. It would seem that the shadow of Joseph Stalin haunts this music.

A poetic link

Pushkin (1799–1837) is a Russian author and poet of the Romantic period. His work established him as the founder of modern Russian literature.

First section (start to fig. 111)

After the tranquil close to the Largo, the finale begins with a surging crescendo. Woodwind trills create a vivid sense of alarm, and the brass (who were silent throughout the third movement) immediately present the main march-like theme:

This will appear many times during the finale. Note the tonic-dominant timpani part that echoes the parody of a march in the first movement (fig. 27).

A second part to the march is introduced at fig. 98 on the first violins (doubled by flute and clarinets) at a somewhat faster tempo. Repeating quavers in the accompaniment (initially including accented and staccato horns) create intense forward momentum, as though the music is driving forwards in an unstoppable fashion.

The opening to the march is blasted out at fig. 100 in the bass register, with bass trombone and tuba giving real force and menace to the sound. In a high register above, the note A is emphasised, decorated in a driving semiquaver figuration by upper strings and some woodwind, and just played as accented crotchets by the E♭ clarinet.

Momentum is maintained after fig. 102 by various techniques, including a figure of 4 semiquavers plus 2 repeating quavers played by the strings in octaves; the 2 semiquavers plus a quaver pattern that is familiar from the first movement; and a quick-march bass line of notes a 4th apart alternating in quavers (a fast 'left–right' feel).

At fig. 103 a variant of the march opening is heard on flute, oboes and clarinets. As their role changes to an accompanying reiteration of chords, the melody passes to a lower register in strings and bassoons. Another bass entry of the march, now in E♭ minor, appears on bass trombone and tuba at fig. 104.

An increasingly frenetic linking passage begins at fig. 105. The dynamic is dropped to *p* (and the orchestration to just strings for a few bars), but the driving 2 semiquaver plus a quaver pattern in the violins and the offbeat accompanying chords do little to dilute the tension. The texture soon becomes more elaborate with various strands, none of them in any way bringing an escape from the sense of onward prolusion.

At fig. 108 upper woodwinds and strings scurry feverishly in semiquavers, as a first appearance of the second-subject theme is heard on a solo trumpet, which scythes through the frenzied woodwind and string melee. Amid the great sense of forward momentum, the note E becomes very significant after fig. 109, not least when the xylophone starts to hammer it out *ff* in semiquavers. It will become the dominant of the A major tonality in which this first section will culminate.

The opening section of the finale reaches its climax at fig. 110, as the melody previously heard on a lone trumpet is now taken up by the whole orchestra as some kind of celebratory anthem:

The exuberant wide leaps (especially rising) and the frolicking chromatic triplets in the trumpets suggest great rejoicing, but the mood is short-lived and will not return.

Second section (fig. 111–121)

At fig. 111, the party breaks off on a short dissonant chord for the whole orchestra. There is a loud crash on the tam-tam and a brutal tritone (G♯–D) on the timpani played *fff* in driving quavers. The march theme briefly returns on the brass. Upper winds and strings also hammer out a tritone (B–F). Approaching fig. 112, the 2 quavers plus a crotchet rhythm on a repeating note (a pattern of great importance in the opening movement) returns on the horns and trombones, and the music quickly fades to *p*.

A solo horn provides a recollection of the rejoicing theme (fig. 112) in a rhythmically augmented version, while troubled semitone quavers are played in the violins. It seems that the music is yearning for a return to lost joy.

An impassioned passage follows at fig. 113. Largely scored for the strings, this has some connections with the Largo; for instance, the first violins four bars before fig. 115 have a version of the main 'A' motif from that movement.

From fig. 116 there follows a lengthy passage of remarkable stillness, with a gently pulsating pattern in the first violins. The effect is withdrawn and shadowy. The violin pattern combines a semitone rise and fall with an octave rise and fall; from fig. 120 the octave is in the opposite direction and mimics the accompaniment pattern in Shostakovich's 'Rebirth' mentioned above. The introduction of this figure on the harp, eventually heard over a major chord of B♭, makes for a moment of sweetness.

Third section (fig. 121 to the end)

Over a long dominant pedal (which prepares for a return to the tonic key of D minor), the ominous march theme returns in rhythmic augmentation on clarinet and bassoons. Flutes and oboes join in with a modified version of the theme at fig. 122, and then it is heard again at fig. 123 on low horns and bassoons (including the contra). The same combination presents the theme at fig. 125, now more darkly in F minor.

The violins enter at fig. 126 with repeating quavers, initially on B. Over the next few pages of the score various pitches are played as repeating quavers, until the apparently all-important A is found. At fig. 128 the music changes into ¾ time, almost like a laboured reminder of the Scherzo. Throughout this lengthy section there is a sense of the register of the music rising, and with it the intensity builds. Various melodic lines also ascend, such as the horns at fig. 129 and the trumpets at fig. 130. Bass instruments also drop out.

By the molto ritenuto (after fig. 130), upper winds and strings have slowly climbed to a very high register, and under this the brass now gradually fill in an increasingly dissonant chord that wrenches the music into the tonic major. Listen out for the long, building snare-drum roll that brings the orchestral texture to the boil at this point.

Almost immediately at fig. 131 much of the orchestra begins the long line of A quavers, while the brass play a grandiose version of the march. Timpani and percussion add colour (listen for the rolls on the triangle as well as the clashes of the cymbals); however, there are moments where the dissonance of brass against the omnipresent A quavers suggests something other than convincing triumph. The final bars with accented timpani and *fff* bass drum is mighty, but many are left wondering just what is being said.

Exercise 29

1. How many brass instruments play the opening appearance of the march theme (starting at the end of bar 2)?

2. How does Shostakovich build the sense of forward momentum between fig. 102–110?

3. What elements make the music at fig. 110 sound like a celebration?

4. What features account for the private, hidden feeling of the music in fig. 112–121?

5. When this symphony was first performed, the audience's standing ovation at the end lasted for more than half an hour. What musical features might account for this?

Section C: Historical Study

This final section of Unit 4 requires you to choose one from a list of three potential Areas of Study, in much the same way that a year ago you chose your Area of Study 2 for the AS Unit 1 paper. It has to be one from the following list:

➤ 3a: English choral music in the 20th century

➤ 3b: Chamber music from Mendelssohn to Debussy

➤ 3c: Four decades of jazz and blues 1910 to 1950.

In the exam you will not have access to scores of the works you have studied. There will be two essay questions on each topic, from which you have to answer one.

AQA does not stipulate which pieces to study; for each topic there are many fabulous pieces from which you might choose. This book discusses a selection of suitable works for each topic which may overlap with the music you study in class, or which might provide a reserve of additional pieces for you to consider. Either way, these pages show you the kind of detail you need to know.

Because no specific pieces are set, the questions will be of a more general nature than those on your set work. Nevertheless, you still need to focus on the music itself in your answers in order to get a good mark.

There are essentially two broad types of question the examiners may ask:

➤ The first is to ask you to write an informative programme note on, perhaps, one or two pieces you have studied

➤ The other is to ask you to comment on how one or more of the main elements of music (structure, melody, rhythm, harmony, texture and the use of instruments) was used in your chosen Area of Study.

Area of Study 3a

English choral music in the 20th century

The English choral tradition is a unique strand of western music. Since the time of Handel – whose choral music you may have studied at AS – the choral scene in England flourished, partly due to the tradition of cathedral choirs and partly due to keen amateur choral societies. For much of the 18th and 19th centuries the most important contributions to the choral tradition came from continental composers, with works such as Haydn's *Creation* (1798), Mendelssohn's *Elijah* (1846) and Dvořák's Requiem (1891).

In the 20th century, English composers once more came to the fore, partly inspired by the choral tradition of their native land. There are many pieces you might choose to study for this topic. It would be possible to look at pieces written for liturgical use,

How to approach this topic:

Most of the works you might choose to study for this topic are either long, or complex, or both. There is a lot of wonderful music to enjoy, but for the exam, try to choose fairly succinct passages from each work that clearly represent the style of the music and the techniques the composer uses. This will enable you to write in some detail about the music rather than gloss over much longer sections in a more general way.

Resources

Dream of Gerontius: published by Novello; recommended recording conducted by John Barbirolli (EMI)

Belshazzar's Feast: published by OUP; recommended recording conducted by Andrew Davis (Apex)

War Requiem: published by Boosey and Hawkes; recommended recording conducted by Benjamin Britten (Decca).

ranging from Vaughan Williams' Mass in G minor to the various canticles and anthems written by Howells for the Anglican cathedrals. More recent pieces by John Rutter and Andrew Carter could be incorporated.

The major choral works of the 20th century, however, tend to be concert pieces such as oratorios, Requiems and Mass settings. There are plenty of good choices to be made in this area; this study guide will focus on the following representative sample:

➤ Elgar: *The Dream of Gerontius* (1900)

➤ Walton: *Belshazzar's Feast* (1931)

➤ Britten: *War Requiem* (1962).

Elgar: The Dream of Gerontius

The composer

Edward Elgar (1857–1934) is a pivotal figure in the history of English music: the first English-born composer of international stature since the death of Purcell (1695). Born into a lowly Worcester family, he was largely self-taught, and composed numerous choral works written in the 1890s for English amateur choral societies.

Elgar's major breakthrough came in 1899 with the *Variations on an Original Theme* – popularly known as the *Enigma Variations* – with its much-loved 'Nimrod' variation. *Gerontius* followed the following year: the start of two fertile decades of creative activity of the highest quality for Elgar, in which he wrote a series of masterpieces including symphonies, concertos, and chamber music.

Other choral works by Elgar that you might study for this unit:

The Apostles (1903)

The Kingdom (1906)

The Music Makers (1912)

The Spirit of England (1917).

The last 15 years or so of Elgar's life were less productive. He was devastated by the loss of his wife, Alice, in 1920; also, perhaps, he felt the First World War had changed the world in which he lived and that his music was less welcome. Finally, in 1933 he started work on his third symphony to a commission from the BBC, but he was not destined to complete it, dying from cancer in 1934.

Background to the work

The Dream of Gerontius is a setting of a poem by Cardinal John Newman, a 19th century English theologian of Protestant origin whose religious writings and views became gradually more Catholic until he finally converted to Roman Catholicism, becoming a priest and then, in later life, a cardinal. The poem deals with Catholic ideas of what happens to the soul after death.

Elgar was brought up as a Catholic and there is evidence that he knew Newman's poem at least as early as 1887. When he was commissioned to compose a major new work for the Birmingham Triennial Festival of 1900, he turned to the Newman poem for his text. The work has since become the most highly-regarded of Elgar's choral works. Where some of his earlier works suffer from sub-standard texts, *Gerontius* is full of imaginative images, and the personal yet universal nature of the theme inspired Elgar to write music of profound and powerful quality.

The oratorio requires three soloists; the main role of Gerontius is sung by a tenor. In Part II there is a second role of almost equal importance which is taken by a mezzo-soprano. The bass sings two short but memorable passages in each half: one as the Priest in Part I and the other as the Angel of the Agony in Part II.

A large chorus is required: as well as providing sufficient power for the climactic moments (especially of the host of heaven singing in Part II), Elgar uses many divisions of the chorus, including a semi-chorus.

Perhaps the most significant musical aspect of the work is Elgar's use of the orchestra. In the *Enigma Variations* he had already shown himself to have great originality and flair for the art of orchestration; here his scoring ensures that the emotions of the text are as much expressed by the orchestra as by the singers. The work requires a full Romantic-sized orchestra of triple woodwind, four horns, three trumpets, three trombones, tuba, timpani and percussion, harp, organ and strings.

A guide to the work

The work is 'through-composed' (i.e. there are no breaks between solos, choruses, etc.) in two parts. Throughout there are a series of themes which bind the whole work together in a manner that Elgar may have learned from Wagner's works (Elgar and his wife had five holidays in Germany in the years 1892–1902, including hearing various performances of Wagner's operas).

Part I opens with an orchestral prelude that presents many of the main musical themes of the oratorio. We are then taken to the scene at Gerontius' deathbed. Gerontius knows his demise is imminent (fig. 22), and people around his bed sing prayers on his behalf (fig. 29). With one last wave of fervent energy, Gerontius professes his faith (fig. 40), but he is also in pain (fig. 57) and scared (fig. 58), causing his attendants to redouble the intensity of their prayers (fig. 63). Finally, mid-phrase, Gerontius passes away (fig. 67), and the Priest sings the last rites of the Catholic Church (fig. 68), with the chorus also joining him to wish the soul well on its journey.

The longer Part II opens with a shorter orchestral introduction that conveys a calm, 'other-worldly' feeling. The Soul of Gerontius awakes (fig. 4) and ponders on the nature of this new experience. In due course the Soul hears the singing of the Angel (fig. 11) who is Gerontius' guardian angel. The Soul introduces itself (fig. 17) and the Angel answers some of its questions, leading to a rapturous duet passage (fig. 27). The Angel leads the Soul towards the judgment court (fig. 29) and the Soul hears the terrifying sounds of the demons gathering souls for hell. This leads to a diabolic chorus for the demons (fig. 32).

The demons fade and, after another short conversation between Soul and Angel (fig. 55), we begin to hear the sounds of the Angelicals (fig. 60). The music builds thrillingly as the Soul and Angel reach the threshold of the court (fig. 71) and the music dazzles (in the bright key of C major) as the Angelicals sing out *fff* the words 'Praise to the holiest in the height' (fig. 74). This is the most substantial choral section of the work, and it reaches a majestic conclusion at fig. 100.

The Angel prepares the Soul for its moment of judgement (fig. 102), and then the Angel of the Agony (the bass soloist) pleads for the Soul in front of God (fig. 106). The Soul departs to go before God to be judged (fig. 114) and we hear the echoes of the bereaved attendants back on Earth (fig. 115). We learn of the Soul's fate from the jubilant Angel (fig. 116) who rises to a top A, though this is almost premature: we are yet to hear the musical representation of the Soul's 'glance of God'. This occurs at fig. 120 after an amazing orchestral crescendo, and the Soul returns in transformed state from the experience and prepares for its time in Purgatory. A brief, distant chorus of Souls in Purgatory (fig. 125) links to the final passage of the work: the Angel's Farewell (fig. 126).

Passages to study

Part I

Prelude

The Prelude is a masterclass in orchestration, providing countless examples of Elgar's skill for handling timbre with imagination and precision, not least the opening, unaccompanied melody (usually called the 'Judgement' theme), played by clarinets, bassoons and muted violas.

Clarinets, bassoons, violas

pp

At fig. 2 a new theme is introduced in a series of imitative string entries: a dotted rhythm figure whose rising contour hides the fact that its harmony slips chromatically downwards (see the cello part); this is traditionally called the 'Fear' motif. This is immediately followed by a homophonic passage with a conjunct melodic line in the woodwinds, an idea called the 'Prayer' motif.

Fig. 4 presents a new melodic idea in triple time on a solo viola. Jaeger calls this the 'Sleep' theme, though the accompaniment is based on the 'Fear' motif in the cellos and harp, suggesting a far from carefree sleep.

A scintillating transformation of the 'Prayer' theme occurs at fig. 9, with the melodic line played in dotted minims (in rhythmic augmentation therefore) as the whole orchestra play *fff*. There is some colourful chromatic harmony here, with the second phrase of the passage starting in A minor and immediately using the Neapolitan chord (B♭ major, first inversion), and the section ends

Further reading

For a detailed analysis of the whole work, read *The Dream of Gerontius: Analytical and Descriptive Notes* written by Elgar's close friend, A. J. Jaeger ('Nimrod' of the *Enigma Variations*), written in 1900 and published by Novello in 1974. In this book Jaeger labels many of Elgar's themes for ease of identification; some of these labels are maintained here.

with some rich 'flat side' harmony at fig. 10 with chords of A♭ major, C minor, D♭ major and a dominant 7th on E♭ in third inversion.

From fig. 12 the Prelude is concerned with the 'Committal' theme (later sung to 'Go forth'): a typically Elgarian broad theme characterised by two rising 7ths that reach out yearningly, especially at first when both first and second violins are playing the theme in unison on the G-string. This builds to a thrilling climax and is a top example of Elgar's imaginative use of the full orchestra: at fig. 14 the main theme is on the second violins and cellos in octaves, along with winds, while the first violins and violas have a surging countermelody in triplets with various suspensions.

The climax subsides and the Prelude ends *ppp* with a restatement of the haunting 'Judgement' theme at fig. 20. The initial entry of Gerontius over a soft roll on the timpani, but played with wooden sticks, creates an immediate intensity to the opening scene.

At fig. 66, Gerontius is nearing death and sings 'Novissima hora est' to a delicate accompaniment on the upper strings, and as he wishes for sleep, the 'Sleep' theme starts, again very soft. His last phrase is sung to a descending chromatic harmonic progression and a final sighing appoggiatura marked 'estinto' (extinguished). Note here that those instruments that have been accompanying him, albeit *ppp*, drop out one by one until we are left with his very last moment of breath unaccompanied.

Gerontius dies

After a silent pause, a rich chord at fig. 68 announces the incantation of the Priest delivering the last rites. The chord is rich because it is the chord of the flattened submediant (B♭ major) following on from the previous section which was in D major, and also because of its scoring: clarinets, bassoons, horns and trombones. The Priest intones his Latin words to a monotone in very solemn manner. The underlying chord progression appears, at first, to be in D minor: VI–II^{7}b–Ic, but then resolves onto F major first inversion and from here repeats the pattern as a descending harmonic sequence starting from a chord of A♭, and then again from a chord of G♭. Finally the harmony reaches a chord of V^{7}c and settles into D major at fig. 70.

Clarinets, bassoons and horns

The new section is built on a tonic pedal, over which the Priest sings a lyrical line. There are various expressive features to the melody including leaps up to top E, and chromatic inflection and an appoggiatura on 'Holy Spirit'. Throughout this passage there is a sense of impending climax with the harp playing pulsating crotchets and the second violins playing tremolo. The entry of the chorus transforms the emotional temperature of the music. Initially they sing in declamatory, homophonic style the chord sequence from the start of the last rites section; then, after a huge unison 'go forth!' with an octave leap on C, they embark in contrapuntal style on the grand 'Committal' theme that was previously heard at the climax of the Prelude.

From fig. 74 Elgar constructs a remarkably opulent texture of up to 13 choral parts (including semi-chorus), the bass soloist and sumptuous orchestral writing bringing the first part to a radiant close.

Part II

Approaching the demons

The music leading up to fig. 29 in Part II is lyrical and passionate, indulging in the warm key of E♭ major, but at this point there is a marked change of temperature as the Soul (and audience) catches the first sounds of the demons. After the certain, rich tonality of the previous section, the music is suddenly much more chromatic: descending semitones in the bass and vocal line combined with a spiky leaping figure in the violins, energised by quaver rests and staccato markings. Timpani and tam-tam are used to convey the 'fierce hubbub' and the tritone in the vocal line at 'make me fear' is very evocative. Other colouristic elements include the use of the stick on the timpani, the portrayal of the 'howl' on the clarinets and violas, glissando on the trombones and double basses, and the use of col legno on the violins.

At fig. 31 Elgar suddenly cuts the orchestra under a thrilling top A♭ for the Angel, and then the music rushes forwards ('stringendo sempre') with glissandos into the renowned 'Demons' Chorus'. Again, chromaticism is evident, especially in the orchestra. The music is also rhythmically energised: dotted patterns are frequently used, and at fig. 33 there is a semiquaver figure using ties to create a keen syncopation that will reappear as the countersubject in the forthcoming fugue:

The fugue subject from fig. 35 is dramatic and full of vitality, as are the interjections in the counterpoint, both in the choral writing and the figure in the orchestra of a semiquaver rest followed by three semiquavers, the first of which is marked *sf*. The entry in the sopranos at fig. 37 is marked by a flourish in the piccolo and flute, and a stroke on the tam-tam and bass drum.

The judgement

At the end of the intercession sung on behalf of the Soul by the Angel of the Agony there is a short linking passage for the Soul who sings above a largely whole-tone chord sequence played softly in the orchestra (divisi violas and cellos with tremolo second violins and some winds).

The sense of mystery is sustained by the softest of organ notes (marked *pppp*) and we then hear the distant voices of the attendants around Gerontius' deathbed back on Earth. There is a sense of church music to this short passage: organ, and then largely a capella (unaccompanied) voices with bell-like harp harmonics. To make the link all the more vivid, the harmonic pattern is the same as that which accompanied the last rites at the end of Part I.

'Real time' is suspended here – appropriately so, given where the scene is set – and we first witness the Angel's response to the judgement. She is heralded by an open 5th flourish in the strings and harp, and her short solo here has an impetuous quality due largely to the orchestral writing: a syncopated line in 3rds in the flutes and bassoons and staccato reiterated semiquavers in the strings. The climax is with an 'Alleluia' using an earlier melodic shape but now reworked to include a top A.

As the 'Alleluia' is being sung, the timpani starts a long roll on A, supported by organ pedals. Over this at fig. 118 we hear the 'Judgement' theme, now in homophonic harmony on the full woodwinds and horns. The brass take over and there is a surge of power and momentum in the music with various flourishes in the flutes and violins. At fig. 120 there is a silent pause on the barline – the most pregnant of pauses – before the entire orchestra erupts on a *fff**zp*. In a footnote Elgar explains this – 'At 120 "for one moment" must every instrument exert its fullest force': it is the composer's representation of the 'one moment' in Newman's poem where the Soul sets eyes on God, and thrillingly managed. In an extraordinary entry the tenor launches in *ff* on a top A with the words 'Take me away', and heads off for time in Purgatory:

Conclusion

Space precludes looking at any further passages of this remarkable oratorio here, but if you choose this work as part of your A2 studies you should have time to study much of the score. In particular, Gerontius' statement of belief 'Sanctus fortis ... Firmly I believe' in Part I and the setting of 'Praise to the Holiest' in Part II are worth examining, and do find time to savour the beautiful 'Angel's Farewell' with which the work ends.

The extraordinary climax at fig. 120 was a moment that did not come to Elgar initially: it was Jaeger, his friend and advisor at his publisher's firm Novello, who urged him to revise his initial ideas to create this memorable moment. You may like to read the correspondence between the two men which can be found in Michael Kennedy's book *Portrait of Elgar* (OUP 1993).

Walton: Belshazzar's Feast

The composer

William Walton (1902–1983) was one of the major composers in English music the generation after Vaughan Williams. Born in Oldham, he was a chorister at Christ Church Cathedral, Oxford, but was largely self-taught as a composer.

The 1930s are, perhaps, the most significant decade of Walton's career. *Belshazzar's Feast* (1930–1931) – a score of extraordinary bravura and colour – launches this period for Walton. Other works of the decade include his Symphony No. 1 (1931–1935), the

Other choral works by Walton that you might study for this unit:

In Honour of the City of London (1937)

Coronation Te Deum (1952–1953)

Gloria (1960–1961).

Web link

A visual representation of this dramatic tale can be seen in Rembrandt's vivid canvas that hangs in the National Gallery and is available online at www.nationalgallery.org.uk

The percussion needs four players in addition to the timpanist, and these players use side drum, tenor drum, triangle, tambourine, castanets, cymbals, bass drum, tam-tam, xylophone, glockenspiel, wood block, slapsticks and an anvil.

haunting Violin Concerto (1936–1939) and his first film scores, the most famous of which – music for Laurence Olivier's film of Shakespeare's *Henry V* – followed in 1943–1944.

Although not hugely prolific, Walton continued to compose into old age and produced a range of works including opera, chamber music, and the coronation marches *Crown Imperial* (1937) and *Orb and Sceptre* (1953).

Background to the work

Belshazzar's Feast is a large-scale cantata (short oratorio) that was commissioned by the BBC and first performed at the Leeds Festival in 1931. Although it lasts little more than 35 minutes, it makes an exhilarating impact on performers and audience alike.

The story of Belshazzar's Feast is found in the Book of Daniel in the Old Testament of the Bible. It concerns a period in ancient history when the Jews had been exiled to Babylon. At a riotous feast held by Belshazzar, King of Babylon, the party is interrupted by the mysterious appearance of a hand, writing on the wall (hence the English expression), casting damning judgment on the King. This story was converted into a libretto for Walton by Osbert Sitwell.

Walton conceived his cantata for enormous forces. Although there is only one vocal soloist, a baritone, the chorus needs to be substantial and is often used as a double choir in eight parts. The orchestration is flamboyant and requires a full Romantic orchestra with triple woodwind including saxophone, a full brass section, an enormous battery of percussion, two harps, piano, organ and strings. In addition, Walton calls for two additional brass bands sat on opposite sides of the stage.

A guide to the work

The cantata falls into four linked sections that suggest a symphonic design.

The first section begins with a striking declamation which sets words of the prophet Isaiah for unaccompanied four-part male chorus (after a brief attention-grabbing blast from three unison trombones). There then follows a lengthy lament, setting words from the Psalms of the Israelites in captivity. This section becomes quite impassioned midway (fig. 9) but ends in introspective and depressed tones.

A link to the next section is provided by a remarkable un-accompanied passage for the solo baritone in the manner of a recitative with a modern twist. In it the wealthy civilisation of Babylon is described in all its pomp and finery.

The second section begins with an instant change of mood at fig. 15. This section is a representation and description of the feast itself. The central focus is an extraordinarily colourful account of the Babylonians praising their 'false gods' of gold, silver, iron, wood and stone. The scene ends with praise of Belshazzar himself.

In the relatively brief third section, a stark contrast is made with some strongly sinister music as the mysterious hand appears and writes Belshazzar's fate on the wall. The passage is framed by more unaccompanied recitative for the baritone, but in an echo of the opening to the cantata, the men of the chorus make the all-important declamation of the judgment.

Almost instantly (fig. 54) the music storms into the final section: an overwhelming chorus of praise to the God of the Israelites. A quieter middle passage from fig. 62 expresses some empathy for the destroyed city of Babylon and provides a musical contrast, but from fig. 67 to the end, there is non-stop rejoicing from the liberated Israelites. Listen out for the final big tune in the basses after fig. 74.

Passages to study

After the introductory page, the mood of lament is quickly established by low tremolo violas and a brooding tune in D minor on the cellos and basses, with an expressive melody that emphasises the minor 3rd before falling to the low tonic. Its unusual rhythmic content creates a sense of ebb and flow, possibly suggesting the waters of Babylon:

Israelites' lament (fig. 1–7)

As the melody ends at fig. 1, the soft but dark timbre of a low D on the bass clarinet and organ pedals, along with a distant roll on the timpani, establishes both the D minor tonality and the air of gloom. The chorus enters and is soon singing a capella with a tonic pedal in the basses and almost wailing melismas in the upper parts on 'waters'. There is a savage dissonance on 'Babylon' with a C minor chord over the D pedal, emphasised with an accent; when the word returns two bars later there is an E♮ in the alto against an E♭ in the soprano.

At fig. 2 the setting of 'Yea, we wept' is highly imaginative: a syncopation to give weight to 'Yea' and then a crunching dissonance on 'wept' with A♭ against A♮. Colouristic touches in the orchestra – pizzicato basses, low piano, timpani and bass drum – are used to depict the heaviest of tears falling to the ground.

The chorus finishes this passage a capella at fig. 3 and the cellos and basses start a short interlude of orchestral music with a sinewy phrase that borders on the atonal. Subsequent entries in the oboe and alto saxophone have sufficient similarity in contour (especially the octave rising leap) to seem imitative. When the chorus re-enters the music begins to pick up tempo, aided by changing time signatures, and there is a sense of antiphony between S/A and T/B voices. The brooding cello melody at fig. 3 with its octave leap is treated to rhythmic diminution in the winds five bars after fig. 4.

After fig. 5 the changes of metre include some bars of $\frac{3}{8}$ time which give an extra impetus to the music. A fast rhythmic figure appears in the orchestra: a triple-tonguing effect on four- or five-note chords in the trumpets and trombones, and a rising three-note figure in the woodwind of two semiquavers and a quaver. Both these patterns are set across the natural triple-time metre at this point; the effect seems to portray a growing sense of hysteria in the Israelites' lament.

The building frenzy in the orchestra (latterly coloured by wooden sticks on the timpani) cuts out suddenly at figure 6 and this passage closes with the chorus alone singing their lament in expressive four-part free counterpoint. The heavily flat-side harmony (the phrase suggests A♭ minor at first), hemiola patterns in the inner parts that create double suspensions, and highly spiced harmony – no more so than at the end on 'in a strange land' – make this a highly affecting a cappella passage.

Praising the Gods (fig. 25–33)

Just before fig. 25 the rest of the orchestra give way to three trumpets and a tambourine to announce the forthcoming declamation from King Belshazzar: a triad of D major is attacked *ffz* and then a crescendo through seven beats culminates in a move upwards to a dissonance for a single beat followed by a long dramatic silence. When the trumpets re-enter they continue the fanfare with detached quavers, accented irregularly, and a final high D major chord which has a crescendo and a flamboyant snare drum role.

There follows a passage of extraordinarily vivid writing as revellers at Belshazzar's Feast praise their various gods. For each one the singers announce the god and then the orchestra reflects the god's character in a brief passage of music: Walton finds dazzling ways of representing the identity of each god in his orchestration. The following table will help show you what to listen for:

Name of god	Choral setting	Orchestral colours
Gold	Solo baritone unaccompanied Repeated by full *ff* homophonic chorus unaccompanied	Full orchestra: entry has maximum impact with *ffp* in brass, and tam-tam and cymbals in support. Moves into grand march after spectacular trill on four horns. Cymbals and bass drum add ceremonial flavour.
Silver	First altos answered by first and second sopranos and second altos	Saxophone solo followed by solo violin. Accompaniment features flutes and piccolo, glockenspiel and triangle, followed by harp harmonics.
Iron	Tenors answered by first and second basses	Muted trombones and stopped (chiuso) horns. Tam-tam played with iron stick and anvil. First appearance of antiphonal brass bands.
Wood	Sopranos and altos in three-part homophony	Strings play col legno (with wood of the bow), plus xylophone and wood block.
Stone	Tenors and basses in three-part homophony	Detached horns and strings with short accented chords supporting slapstick in percussion section.
Brass	Full chorus	*ff* entries from the two brass bands supported with long cymbal roll.

The first of these – the God of Gold – carries the greatest impact. After the dramatic fanfare announcement, the entry of the King, sung by the baritone soloist, is colossal: a huge phrase high in the baritone range with maximum declamatory weight. The quintuplet quavers and triplet minims lend grandeur to the melody, which then reaches top E on 'gold'. The chorus response maintains the intensity of the music with some 'added note' harmony and a spectacular top A for the first sopranos to finish:

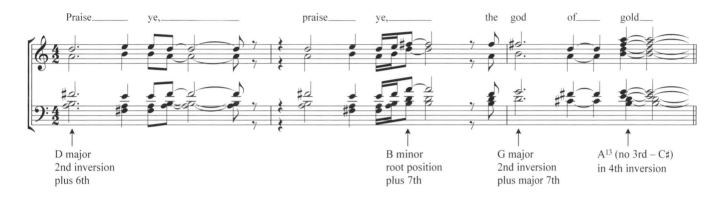

The orchestral reply is glittering. For eight bars there is a sense of suspense as the music moves (with six bars over a supertonic pedal and two bars of dominant harmony) towards a resolution on D major at fig. 27. Here Walton launches into a commanding, if short-lived, full-scale grandiose march. This is the composer using the music of imperial Edwardian Britain (Elgar's *Pomp and Circumstance* style) to portray the decadence of the great Babylonian civilisation, perhaps some kind of semi-political musical satire.

The central dramatic scene of the story is treated with marked economy by Walton, but also with highly imaginative and dramatic scoring.

The writing on the wall (fig. 52–54)

The scene is set by a short section of unaccompanied recitative for the baritone soloist. The melodic contour here is highly expressive; in particular note that:

➢ The opening suggests the darkness of a minor tonality (G minor)

➢ There is a melismatic flourish on 'feasted'

➢ The unexpected rising major 7th for 'man's hand' conveys a sense of mystery and creepiness

➢ The melody plummets dramatically at the end with a falling minor 7th, which creates an ominous feel.

After a pregnant pause, the orchestra creates a mood of intense suspense. A four-note falling motif in the contrabassoon, double

basses and low in the piano suggests doom; this is heard against a backdrop of low tremolo and four-note chord in the cellos and harps. The cellos play *sul ponticello* (bowed on the bridge) and the harps *près de la table* (plucked at the bottom of the string by the soundboard), both colouristic techniques that create a rather ghostly sound. Finally, the percussion writing is immensely imaginative: a long sustained **pp** roll on the tenor drum, soft strokes on cymbals, bass drum and tam-tam, and the sporadic twitch of the castanets. The overall musical canvas vividly suggests a frighteningly creepy desert scene.

	Beat 1	Beat 2	Beat 3	Beat 4
Tenor drum	roll	roll	roll	roll
Timpani			✓	
Castanets		✓		offbeat ✓
Tam-tam				✓
Cymbals	✓			
Bass drum		✓		

Against this backdrop the baritone continues his narration of the scene, intoning in a quasi-speech rhythm on a low, dark B♭. Grating, throbbing semitones occur on the whining timbre of high bassoons and two solo violas. The baritone sings the Hebrew words that the mysterious hand writes: 'Mene, mene, tekel, upharsin', and a trill on flute and piccolo, ending with a rising chromatic scale, adds to our suspense.

In an echo of how the cantata opened, unison trombones sound and the tenors and basses in four-part dissonant harmony intone the translation of the Hebrew words in declamatory style. The baritone solo announces the death of the King with one last ostentatious melisma on 'Belshazzar', and the chorus repeats the word 'slain' to a spectacular shout. The final line 'and his kingdom divided' seems to represent a sense of Belshazzar's regime splitting apart through the breaking of the F♯ minor pattern by a final C♮ (achieved by a fall of an augmented 4th) rather than the expected C♯. It also links with what follows since the C♮ is the dominant note of the final 'movement' of the cantata.

Final paean of praise (fig. 74 to the end)

The final pages of the cantata are a tumult of festive music on a grand scale, as the Israelites celebrate their liberation. At fig. 74 there is a short break in the music to articulate the start of the final passage. At this point Walton uses a composite time signature. The music is essentially in a quadruple metre (four beats) which is notated in the choral parts as $\frac{4}{2}$ time. However, such is the fervour of the music in the orchestra that each of these beats is treated as a bar of $\frac{3}{8}$ by the orchestral players.

In this extraordinarily vibrant and full texture, the main melody comes in the chorus basses, supported by the trombones: a grand theme of noble character set against sustained chords in the upper chorus parts.

Then sing a - loud_____ To God our strength_____

Meanwhile the woodwind, trumpets and snare drum dazzle with an ostinato rhythm in the brisk compound metre and the upper strings play scurrying scales. The whole texture is supported by a huge tonic pedal, not least on the pedals of the organ itself. After four phrases of the the main melody in the bass, the theme is taken up by the tenors, supported by the horns. The tenors' second phrase reaches a climactic top A, the sopranos go one better with a high B♭, and – at fig. 76 – the passage cadences on the tonic.

The remaining pages form a coda. All parts are now in fast compound time; the changing number of beats in the bar maintain the excited energy of the music. Though the full orchestra is engaged, the texture is somewhat simpler. From fig. 76 many instruments are hammering out rhythms on the tonic note F, and from fig. 81 this changes to the dominant note C. Walton writes antiphonally for the two choruses from just before fig. 77 and they exchange alleluias. From about this point the two antiphonal brass bands also join the party. Listen for the flamboyant glissandos in the harps. The final alleluia is sung by both choruses as the orchestra is silent for two bars. The orchestra then re-enters for a brief postlude in which Walton punctuates tonic chords with silences. There is a triplet anacrusis to the final chord, which is played by full orchestra and both brass bands; full organ joins the chord two bars later and the chord stops with a final cymbal crash.

Conclusion

Despite its relative brevity (compared to *Gerontius,* for example), *Belshazzar's Feast* is a choral work of huge impact. Throughout Walton shows a deep instinct for choral writing, born of his years as a chorister at Oxford, and the orchestra writing is consistently brilliant. The size of forces required for the work mean that it is well worth attending a live performance for the full impact of the music to be appreciated.

Britten: War Requiem

The composer

Benjamin Britten (1913–1976) is arguably the most significant English composer of the middle of the 20th century. He was born in Lowestoft on the Suffolk coast, a location that inspired many of his works. He showed early musical creative talent, writing over 100 pieces before he was 14, at which point he started to visit London for composition lessons with Frank Bridge, winning a scholarship to the Royal College of Music in 1930.

Career opportunities, as well as the prospect of looming war in Europe (Britten was a pacifist) led Britten to move to America in

April 1939 where he wrote various works including the *Sinfonia da Requiem* and a Violin Concerto. He also began a lifelong relationship with the singer Peter Pears.

Britten returned to England in 1942, pursuing a highly successful creative career. Projects often involved working with amateur musicians, especially children, but he also wrote for many eminent musicians of his day. His most significant field of work, however, was opera: he more or less single-handedly revived English opera, which had lain virtually dormant since Purcell's *Dido and Aeneas* (c. 1689).

Other choral works by Britten that you might study for this unit:

Saint Nicolas (1947–1948)

Spring Symphony (1948–1949)

Cantata academica (1959).

Background to the work

The industrial city of Coventry was decimated by 515 German bombers on the night of 14th November 1940. Among the ruins the following morning was the old cathedral. After the war a new cathedral was built next to the ruins of the old one; it was consecrated on 25th May 1962. As part of the rebuild project, Britten was commissioned to write a new work.

He was an interesting choice because of his pacifist views, and he chose to write a large-scale setting of the ancient Latin Requiem text interspersed with some of the poetry written in the trenches of the First World War by Wilfred Owen. The piece makes use of the space of the new Coventry Cathedral: a large main chorus, who – along with a soprano soloist – sing the words of the Mass, is accompanied by a large orchestra (triple wind, six horns, and triple brass, four percussionists, etc.) and a large organ; two further soloists – tenor and baritone – sing Owen's poetry accompanied by a chamber orchestra; finally, a boys' choir sing at some further distance, accompanied mainly by a chamber organ.

Wilfred Owen, perhaps the greatest of the so-called 'war poets', was killed at the front line a week before the end of the First World War in 1918. Britten headed his score with Owen's lines: 'My subject is War, and the pity of War. The Poetry is in the pity… All a poet can do today is warn'.

Britten intended the opening performance to convey a spirit of reconciliation and to this end wanted the three soloists to be Russian, German and British. Unfortunately the Russian soprano was forbidden to travel for the performance by the Russian Ministry of Culture. However, Britten later recorded the work with his full first-choice team.

> **Resources**
>
> For detailed background and analysis of the work see Mervyn Cooke: *Britten War Requiem* (Cambridge Music Handbooks 2008).

Passages to study

Requiem aeternam (complete)

The *War Requiem* opens with cold and dark sounds: a single stroke on a gong, followed by a lugubrious wheeze from the orchestra. An F♯ bell starts to toll and the sopranos and tenors softly intone the words 'requiem aeternum' ('eternal rest') to a low F♯. The whole orchestra then plays a phrase built on the initial 'wheeze' figure. There is a laboured, weary feel to the music, due to the very slow tempo and the unusual subdivision of the beat into five. Another bell is heard – a C – and the altos and basses now intone to this note: a tritone away from the sopranos' and tenors' F♯.

This interval of a tritone is of central importance to the work. Long ago it was known as *diabolus in musica* (the devil in music) and its harsh, jarring sound is particularly suited to Britten's theme for this Requiem. It is as though the two notes represent the opposing factions of the war and together they depict its terror and ugliness.

Over the next few entries the two notes get closer together until they are heard in conflict simultaneously. Meanwhile, the orchestral phrases between the choral entries become progressively heavier and more insistent with the ominous colours of the gong and the bells to the fore. Finally the passage fades away towards fig. 3.

At fig. 3 the boys' choir make a first appearance, accompanied by organ, and sing the Latin hymn 'Te decet hymnus'. The sense of conflict persists: the first phrase for the higher voices (one note short of being a 12-tone melody: there's no G♮) is repeated by the lower voices, but inverted and starting a tritone lower:

Meanwhile the first and second violins of the main orchestra alternate **pp** sustained high Cs and F♯s, bringing a sense of chill to the music.

This passage becomes fragmentary as fig. 7 is approached and, in the end, only the tritone is left. This interval is then, once more, taken up by the bells and the main chorus as a third section (very much like the first) gets under way. This lasts through to fig. 9.

At this point we hear for the first time the words of Wilfred Owen set for the tenor soloist accompanied by the chamber orchestra. There are several elements here which create a vivid atmosphere:

➢ The harp figuration which is built around the tritone interval (now spelled G♭–C)

➢ The military associations of the drums (bass drum with wooden sticks and side drum without snare)

➢ The march-like dotted rhythms in the strings

➢ The often dissonant duet writing for the woodwind (initially flute and clarinet, later oboe and bassoon) which, while having the same rhythm, is often a 7th or 9th apart.

Also, notice how the tenor solo line is largely syllabic, except for the melisma on 'wailing'.

At fig. 13 Britten responds to the line 'not in the hands of boys' by quoting the melody the boys' choir sang for 'Te decet' in the woodwind: a solo oboe answered by a clarinet. In an imaginative use of timbre, both are doubled by the ghostly sound of sul ponticello violins. Similarly, a solo horn is doubled by pizzicato second violins before fig. 14, and then, five bars before fig. 15, the bassoon has the inverted version of the 'Te decet' tune, once again doubled by sul ponticello violins.

As the chamber orchestra finish at fig. 16, the tritone bells of the main orchestra sound again. The movement ends with the main chorus singing the Kyrie in a simple homophonic setting in which the harmony is sombre and dark with various dissonances, ending on a consonant chord of F major, which does not entirely settle the sense of unease.

Dies irae (up to fig. 22)

From the outset, Britten's setting of the Dies irae – 'Day of wrath' – fuses the religious imagery of God's anger on the day of judgement with the battlefield. The movement begins with distant sounds of brass instruments playing battle-calls. The fact that these are tonally unrelated (the trombone plays a G major arpeggio, the trumpet a B♭ major arpeggio, and the horn a D♭ minor arpeggio, with a major 7th to finish on) conveys a sense of disunity.

After a little more disjointed brass, the main material of the movement appears: a threatening idea in $\frac{7}{4}$, punctuated with crotchet rests. The accompaniment is designed to dovetail with this:

The rising scale at the end of this example is particularly menacing: it continues the brittle, short style of singing, but both the E♭ at the bottom and the D♭ at the top of the scale are dissonant with the bass, and the crescendo conveys a sense of horror which is reinforced by the bass drum roll in the next bar.

After an interlude of further brass calls, the tonal centre of the music moves to A for the second verse of the text which is sung by the upper voices of the chorus with a fuller texture in the orchestra.

The next interlude – prior to the words 'Tuba mirum spargens sonum' ('the trumpet pouring forth its awful sound') – is the most apocalyptic yet: the entire brass complement of six horns, four trumpets, three trombones and tuba participate, often *ff*, and timpani, bass drum and contrabassoon provide additional thunderous effects. When the chorus enters it is in a suitably forceful manner (marked 'heavy'). The climax of the verse is reinforced by timpani, bass drum, tenor drum and cymbals.

Sanctus (up to fig. 87)

The Sanctus opens with the sound of bells – vibraphone, glockenspiel, antique cymbals, bells and high piano – playing F♯ with a crescendo from *pp* to *f*. The soprano soloist then declaims the word 'Sanctus' ('Holy'). This happens twice and then a more metrical phrase follows in which the bell sounds beat rhythmically and the soprano has a long melisma on 'Sanctus':

San - - - - - - - ctus

At fig. 84 a similar passage to the music so far described begins. Now, however, the bells play C; the troubling, dark tritone interval that dominated the work's opening movement is still colouring the music, despite the Sanctus traditionally being seen as a picture of heaven.

The chorus enters at fig. 85 in one of the most visionary passages of the whole score. In eight parts they chant the text 'Pleni sunt caeli et terra gloria tua' ('Heaven and earth are full of thy glory') to a free rhythm on a series of overlapping monotones. This starts *pp* on a low F♯ in the second basses; in each subsequent bar another part enters on another note, and sometimes a part that has already been singing on one pitch leapfrogs others and provides the next new entry. Each pitch the choir adds to the texture is reinforced by tremolo strings and trilling woodwind.

The overall effect is extraordinary: the texture fills, the pitch ascends, and the dynamic builds to *ff*. Over the course of the passage the chanting is heard on all 12 degrees of the chromatic scale at some point in the texture. Try to imagine this live in a large building with a ringing acoustic – like Coventry Cathedral – the whole place would fill with sound, thereby reflecting the meaning of the words.

The first half of this movement contains some shatteringly powerful music. At fig. 118 Britten turns again to the Owen war poetry and a haunting poem of two dead soldiers from opposing sides talking to each other. This he sets for the tenor and baritone soloists accompanied by the chamber orchestra. The use of timbre here is remarkable and chilling; among the effects to listen out for are:

Libera me (fig. 118 to the end)

➤ The sustained chords on the strings – marked 'cold' they are played without vibrato

➤ The use of double bass harmonics

➤ The careful deployment of wind instruments to subtly change the tone colour and free the upper strings for other roles; look out particularly for the use of low flute notes

➤ The surges of upper strings (e.g. fig. 119) played with vibrato and an up-bow to allow for increasing bow pressure; often the more whining timbre of the viola is used at the top

➤ The use of bass drum and double bass at fig. 120 to colour the mention of 'guns thumped'

➤ The use of the harp in response to 'wildest beauty' at fig. 122.

With the utmost poignancy, the baritone sings unaccompanied before fig. 127 when explaining his identity to the other soldier.

From fig. 127 the music suggests reconciliation: the protagonists sing together 'Let us sleep now', while the boys' choir sings the final words of the Requiem text 'In paradisum'. There is a luminescence to the music: D is established as a key centre and the effect is major, though with G♯s in the key signature there is a suggestion of the bright Lydian mode (with a sharpened 4th). Much of this passage is built over a stable tonic pedal.

The main chorus joins in after fig. 131 and Britten controls the three groups of musicians consummately. It is hard to imagine the effect just from stereo speakers or headphones but live, in a large cathedral, this is music of spine-tingling beauty. The peak of the passage is the soprano soloist's top B, six bars before fig. 135, which is further enhanced by being at the moment a roll of a suspended cymbal reaches its pinnacle.

Just when the work seems to have reached its fulfilment of peace, security and tranquillity, Britten once more returns to the menace of the tritone which is played by the bells at fig. 135 and cuts off the flow of all the other musicians. The boys intone on the tritone too, before other musicians try to resume their uplifting hymn. However, the music has given up its certainty and there is a further interjection of the bells and the boys' choir with the tritone.

After a final echo of the 'let us sleep now' music, the *War Requiem* ends uneasily with the choir singing 'Requiescant in pace, Amen' to music similar to the end of the work's first movement. The final tritone of the bells is heard four bars before the end. The last *pppp* F major chord from the choir has a sense of peace, but is also unexpected after so much music based on D, and makes a thought-provoking effect on the audience.

Conclusion

The *War Requiem* is a unique concept for a choral work and inspired the pacifist Britten to write one of his most powerful scores. His use of different texts, different groups of musicians, and the space afforded by the new cathedral for which it was written is highly imaginative and skilfully realised. From a purely choral point of view, the score includes many original responses to the challenge of writing for chorus. It is undoubtedly one of the most significant works in the English choral tradition.

Area of Study 3b

Chamber music from Mendelssohn to Debussy

The Classical period composers – such as Haydn, Mozart, and Beethoven – established chamber music as one of the great genres of music, especially with their string quartets. As European society became more bourgeois and people had money to give themselves leisure time, so the demand for chamber music increased through the 19th century.

As the musical language of the century became more Romantic, so the chamber music of the period changed. Sometimes this is reflected in the number of players required: Haydn had invented the string quartet; now composers sometimes wrote for larger groups. Mendelssohn wrote his remarkable String Octet in 1825, while still only 16 years old. Developments in instruments also opened up new possibilities; in particular it was the century in which the piano came of age and composers were quick to explore the potential of writing for groups of several instruments plus piano. Finally, various traits that motivated the Romantic composers – emotion, national identity, chromatic harmony, virtuosity, etc. – all find expression in the chamber music you might study for this topic.

The most important composers who wrote chamber music in this period are Mendelssohn, Schumann, Brahms, Dvořák, Tchaikovsky, Saint-Saëns, Fauré, Ravel and Debussy.

This study guide will focus on the following representative movements:

➤ Mendelssohn: Piano Trio No. 1 in D minor Op. 49, third movement (1839)

➤ Schumann: Piano Quartet in E♭, third movement (1842)

➤ Brahms: Piano Quintet in F minor Op. 34, third movement (1862)

➤ Tchaikovsky: String Quartet No. 2 in F Op. 22, second movement (1874)

➤ Dvořák: Piano Quintet in A Op. 81, second movement (1887)

➤ Debussy: String Quartet in G minor, second movement (1893).

Mendelssohn: Piano Trio in D minor Op. 49, third movement – Scherzo

The scherzo is often associated with Beethoven, who is renowned for writing scherzos that have a stormy nature (for example, the second movement of his ninth symphony). Mendelssohn, however, took a different approach: a lightweight, delicate type of movement, famously seen in the 'fairy-like' Scherzo he wrote for the incidental music to *A Midsummer Night's Dream*.

How to approach this topic:

Most of the works you might choose to study are quite substantial and have several (usually four) movements. There is a lot of wonderful music to enjoy, but insofar as the exam is concerned, try to choose individual movements from works that clearly represent the style and the techniques each composer uses. This will enable you to write in some detail about the music without needing to know complete works thoroughly.

The main categories of ensemble:

String quartet: 2 violins, viola, cello

String quintet: 2 violins, 2 violas, cello *or* 2 violins, 1 viola, 2 cellos

String sextet: 2 violins, 2 violas, 2 cellos

String octet: 4 violins, 2 violas, 2 cellos

Piano trio: violin, cello, piano

Piano quartet: violin, viola, cello, piano

Piano quintet: 2 violins, viola, cello, piano

Clarinet quintet: clarinet, 2 violins, viola, cello.

Web link

Scores for many of these works can be downloaded at http://imslp.org

A valuable subscription resource for recordings is www.naxosmusiclibrary.com

The scherzo from the D minor Piano Trio is very much in this mode. As a pianist Mendelssohn was admired for his light staccato touch, which is apparent from the start of this movement. Such is the silky smoothness of the movement's rapid flow that the piece may at first appear seamless; however, there is a structure that is essentially sonata form:

Bars 1–47	Exposition	Bars 1–8: statement of first subject in D major in piano only.
		Bars 8–28: Transition starting with restatement of first subject in violin; modulation to V starts around bar 13.
		Bars 28–38: second subject in A major.
		Bars 39–47: codetta, returning to I.
Bars 47–117	Development	Bars 47–54: development starts with a restatement of first subject in I by the piano, which ends with a shift towards E minor.
		Bars 54–71: the music explores a series of minor keys (E, B, F♯) as Mendelssohn develops the first subject.
		Bars 82–100: this passage makes considerable use of contrasting dynamics with pairs of bars alternating between loud and soft. A louder and longer phrase starts at bar 92 as the music moves towards F♯ minor.
		Bars 100–117: the sudden return to $\boldsymbol{pp}$ at bar 100 in the relative of the dominant creates a sense of expectation and the music is propelled towards the recap, though without any great build-up of dynamic or texture.
Bars 118–172	Recapitulation	Bars 118–141: recapitulation of first subject in violin (with counterpoint of semiquavers in piano right hand) moving seamlessly into re-written transition. The idea from bar 17, previously in A, is now in the tonic at bar 128.
		Bars 141–172: recapitulation and extension of second subject now in D.
Bars 172–188	Coda	Alternating piano and strings for four bars; then the opening bar from the first subject is used from bar 176. The movement ends with a final flourish from the piano and a very light perfect cadence.

The opening melody sets the character of this light, yet spirited movement; the rhythm of its first half-bar pervades much of the piece and the grouping of two semiquavers followed by a quaver is used to create an energetic cross-rhythm prior to the entry of the strings (bars 6–7). The theme is unusual for having asymmetric phrases: a three-bar statement followed by a four-bar answer.

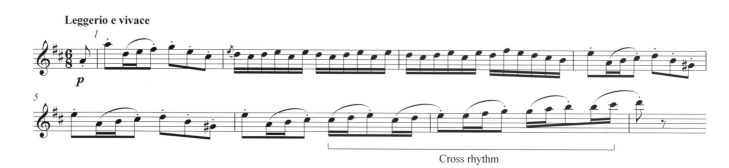

Cross rhythm

The rising semiquaver figuration in 6ths between the hands (bars 17–18 and 23–24) creates a very buoyant effect, as does the rising chromatic scale in bars 26–27. The second subject is a delicate affair punctuated by quaver rests. Its contour is largely built from falling conjunct motion.

Mendelssohn's use of texture in the movement is usually light, but there is some charming variety of textures. In particular, listen out for:

➢ Alternating half bars between the strings and the piano at bars 13–15

➢ The violin presenting the second subject, answered by the cello (bars 28–34)

➢ Alternating bars between piano and the strings at bars 38–41

➢ Piano semiquavers doubled a 6th lower by the violin in bars 56–60

➢ A set of four imitative entries (piano R.H., piano L.H., violin, cello) from bar 63

➢ The violin and cello in imitation at bars 73–77

➢ Double octaves in the piano's diminished 7th falling arpeggio at bars 135–136.

The harmonic palette of the movement is clearly tonal, but there are plenty of deft chromatic touches to add a little spice. Among those to note are:

➢ Bar 4: After three bars of essentially tonic (D major) harmony, the first subject counterbalances this in standard classical manner by basing the answering phrase on the dominant; however, this is coloured by chords of the tonic minor and dominant of the dominant in the second half of bar 4 and 5.

➢ Bars 25–26: A good example of Mendelssohn's frequent use of secondary 7ths: the B minor chord on bar 25^1 (chord II in the new key of A major) is preceded with its dominant ($F\sharp^7$ in first inversion); similarly the chord of F♯ minor on bar 26^1 (chord VI) is preceded by its dominant ($C\sharp^7$ first inversion) at bar 25^4.

➢ Bars 35–40: A good area for understanding the Romantic composers' liking for the diminished 7th. In bar 35–36 the harmony is essentially a chord of B^7 acting as a dominant to the chord of E major at bar 37^1. However, the B keeps changing to a C♮, thereby creating a diminished 7th chord. Similarly in bars 38 and 40, the diminished 7th chord on the second quaver is a dominant 7th to the chord that follows.

➢ Bars 98–101: This climactic moment of the development section comprises a virtuoso arpeggio on an augmented 6th chord (German variety) which, like nearly all such chords, precedes a dominant chord (C♯ major – we're in F♯ minor at this point). Another German 6th occurs in bar 111, and Italian 6ths can be found on the last quaver of bars 172 and 174 in the codetta.

Schumann: Piano Quartet in E♭, third movement – Andante cantabile

1842–1843: Schumann's chamber music year

Schumann wrote many of his most important chamber works within a very concentrated period: three string quartets Op. 41, the piano quartet and piano quintet all date from 1842.

For the majority of Classical and early Romantic four-movement works, the slow movement is placed second, followed by a menuet and trio, or a scherzo (as in the Mendelssohn Piano Trio above). One trait of 19th-century music, however, was its expressive melodic lyricism. The more this flourished, the stronger was the urge to make the slow movement the heart of a work and place it third. Few composers of the day were more romantic in their outlook than Schumann, and therefore it is no surprise to find this exquisite andante placed third in his Piano Quartet.

The movement is essentially in ternary form. There is a strong contrast between the 'A' and 'B' sections:

A sections	B section
B♭ major ¾	G♭ major ⁴⁄₄
Melody-dominated texture with some use of free counterpoint for countermelodies	A more chordal, homophonic texture

Note the quaver appoggiatura on the downbeat of bar 4 at the close of the violin's introductory melodic phrase: Schumann's melodic writing is full of such moments.

The shortest of introductions starts with a resolute diminished 7th chord which fades from *f* to *p* as it resolves onto the dominant (F major). This is not such a surprise: the diminished 7th is really a dominant 7th on C (i.e. V of V), in which the root C is swapped for D♭ (the minor 9th). In bar 2 the rising leap of a major 10th sets the character for the main theme which starts in bar 3 in the cello.

This is one of Schumann's most beautiful melodies and is particularly suited to the warm tone of the cello. The theme is built from a four-bar phrase that is treated as a falling sequence. The phrase has an exquisite shape: conjunct save for a rising 7th in its second bar and a falling 7th in its final bar. These 7ths suffuse the whole movement and give a very rich, yearning feel to the music.

On its first statement the melody is accompanied by a strong harmonic progression in the piano, chords reiterated in quavers and single notes on the third beat of each bar in the viola and violin. Before the cello has completed the final phrase, the violin enters with a restatement of the theme two octaves higher where the violin's timbre is at its sweetest. Piano and viola continue to provide accompaniment in the same manner as before; the cello, however, provides a countermelody to the violin in its tenor register. This uses similar melodic shapes, but overlaps its phrases with the violin's theme.

The remainder of the opening 'A' section takes the form of a dialogue between the piano and the viola. The piano melody, which is in even quavers, is all displaced by a semiquaver, creating constant syncopation.

At bar 47 all four instruments in unison link to the new key of G♭ major, simply by descending in steps down to the new tonic. The 'B' section is serene and lacks the yearning 7ths in the melody. The choice of key aids that intimate mood since no open strings are available to the string players. The return to B♭ for the reprise of the 'A' material is just as simple as the previous change of key: all instruments in unison slip down G♭ to F and this – the dominant of B♭ – allows for the return of the opening theme.

This time the viola plays the theme (in the octave between that in which the cello and violin previously played it) and the piano chordal pattern is somewhat different. An extra element is the line of flowing semiquavers in the violin. During the passage the cellist is given rest in order to re-tune the C-string down to B♭ for the final pedal note.

This time Schumann extends the 'A' section at bar 90 with a variant on his main theme in the violin that also uses sequence. The viola imitates the violin two bars later and the two play interweaving phrases. Meanwhile the semiquaver countermelody passes to the piano.

The 'A' section really finishes with the perfect cadence into bar 105 where a coda starts. This occurs over a tonic pedal B♭, firstly in the piano and latterly in the cello (using the re-tuned bottom string). For the first half of the coda the cello is given the theme again while the other two strings have long sustained notes.

Brahms: Piano Quintet in F minor Op. 34, third movement – Scherzo

Brahms arguably made the most significant contribution to chamber music in the 19th century; the Piano Quintet in F minor is one of the pinnacles of the genre and one of several chamber works he wrote in the early 1860s.

This scherzo movement has a fiery, brooding character that makes a strong contrast with the Mendelssohn scherzo examined above. This is gained through a driving sense of rhythm throughout much of the outer sections, which are in C minor and duple time (with some sections in $\frac{2}{4}$ and some in $\frac{6}{8}$). The middle section ('Trio') is in the tonic major and rather more lyrical in character.

The main scherzo (the 'A' section) is built around three ideas:

➢ A: The opening theme (see overleaf) – a melody that stretches upwards with a sense of urgency due to the syncopated initial rising arpeggio pattern. Also highly significant is the figure of a rising 3rd which is treated in rising sequence in bars 9–11.

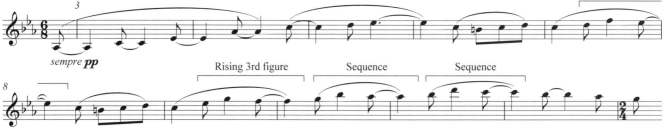

➤ B: The melody in the $\frac{2}{4}$ section played by first violin and doubled an octave lower by viola built from a note repeated in dotted rhythm and a four-note semiquaver turn figure.

➤ C: The march-like homophonic material in major mode that is mainly full chords played as dotted crotchets.

The structure of the 'A' section is as follows:

Bars 1–12	A	Presented in octaves by first violin and viola in C minor and played ***pp***; partially imitative countermelody in piano; tonic pedal in cello
Bars 13–21	B	Initially just the melody in octaves (first violin and viola); latterly with pizzicato chords. In C minor, but based around the fifth degree (G)
Bars 22–45	C	A full-blooded statement ***ff*** in C major, that finishes with references to 'A' back in C minor
Bars 46–57	A	Similar to before but changing in bar 52 to move towards G minor. Played ***pp*** again. Rising 3rd figure still treated to rising sequence bars 53–56
Bars 57–67	B	Now presented ***ff*** by the full ensemble. Bars 57–60 are in G minor, then the music moves to B♭ minor
Bars 67–109	B	The $\frac{2}{4}$ material is now treated to a fugal development with entries on B♭ in the viola (bar 67), E♭ in the piano (bar 71), B♭ in the violin (bar 76), E♭ back in the piano (bar 80), B♭ in the viola (bar 84) and A♭ in the violin (bar 88). A countersubject is constructed from a syncopated falling conjunct pattern. The passage ends in a unison statement B in all parts except the right hand of the piano which provides an energetic foil to the theme
Bars 109–144	C	Another full ***ff*** statement now in E♭ major, again finishing with references to 'A' in E♭ minor and then in C minor (from bar 134)
Bars 144–157	A	The start of the final climactic passage of the scherzo section: 'A' now played ***ff*** for the first time. Rising 3rd figure now treated to thrilling falling sequence
Bars 158–193	B	An extended passage based on 'B' and played ***ff*** for maximum rhythmic drive and intensity

While following this muscular movement, listen for the following details:

➤ The foreshadowing of 'C' in the accompanying chords immediately before this idea (bars 18–21) while the music is still in C minor.

➤ The use of secondary 7ths in 'C', bars 26–29.

➢ The harmony at bars 39–40 where an augmented 6th chord is used in first inversion; the A♭ and F♯ have the effect of closing in on the dominant G as the music returns to C minor from C major.

➢ The texture used in bars 146–157: with the piano thundering out octaves deep in the bass, all string instruments, including the cello, combine in playing the melodic material in a series of doublings; particularly Brahmsian are bars 154–157 where cello and viola are in 3rds, with second violin an octave above the cello, and with the first violin two octaves above the viola. Meanwhile the piano right hand plays a countermelody in octaves.

➢ Use of Neapolitan harmony (D♭ major chord) in the piano, bars 177–183.

The Trio section, like the Scherzo, opens with a tonic pedal in the cello, but the darkness and agitation of the Scherzo has been left behind. The main theme in the piano is initially legato and has a beautiful rising contour that is mostly conjunct or uses 3rds. Around the ninth bar of the melody the music moves to the dominant; there is then a further, more surprising move towards the remote key of B major (bars 206–209), before returning to a G chord which now takes an F♮, ready to return to C. The melody is immediately repeated by the strings with the piano providing discreet arpeggios. The harmonisation is somewhat different: the tonic pedal disappears and Brahms uses the circle of 5ths in bars 213–219.

There is a brief middle section to the Trio (bar 226–241). Over a dominant pedal in the piano, the violins in octaves play what appears to be a new melody that regularly climbs a 3rd and falls a 2nd. In fact this three-note shape is taken from the 'A' idea of the Scherzo as marked in the example on the previous page. There is a sense of increasing energy as the middle note in the pattern becomes increasingly shorter. From bar 233 the texture is swapped around and the violins' tune appears in the left hand of the piano while the cello plays the dominant pedal.

The final passage returns to the Trio's main theme, which is again in the strings. It is altered towards the end to avoid the move to B major, instead coming to rest on the tonic. The harmonisation of this tune is again different and starts with a rather surprising B♭ in the bass of the piano, which then sinks mainly by step to C.

Tchaikovsky: String Quartet No. 2 in F major Op. 22, second movement – Scherzo

Russia's tradition of art music goes back less far into the country's history than elsewhere in Europe: various factors, especially a political one with the rule of the Tsars, meant that the Russian society was slow to develop a middle class. However, by the second half of the 19th century this was changing, so new opportunities for musicians emerged; Tchaikovsky's second string quartet was first played in a private evening recital.

This Scherzo movement is in D♭ major: a major 3rd away from the key of the first movement (the tonic of the first movement is now the mediant in this movement). The overall effect of the movement is far less boisterous than Mendelssohn's Scherzo discussed above; indeed, this is a rather delicate movement with considerable poise, as might be expected from a composer famed for his ballet music.

The structure of the movement is a standard ternary form in which virtually the whole of the 'A' section is repeated note-for-note after the 'B' section (Trio) before being extended with a coda.

The 'A' section is itself in a tripartite form: the main theme is presented in bars 1–30, ending on the dominant; bars 31–69 provide a middle section, before a restatement of the opening theme starts at bar 70. This is identical for 20 bars until a slight extension enables the section to end on the tonic.

The main quirky element that warrants the title 'Scherzo' is rhythmic: in particular the composer's treatment of metre. Tchaikovsky mixes bars of 6/8 (effectively two beats) with bars of 9/8 (three beats) to create asymmetric patterns. For much of the movement two bars of 6/8 are followed by one of 9/8, thereby producing the illusion of a metre with seven beats:

The sense of seven in this movement makes a fascinating comparison with the second movement of Tchaikovsky's sixth symphony, which is in 5/4.

From the start we hear seven such phrases, before Tchaikovsky teases the listener's expectations by having a phrase of 9 beats followed by one of 11 beats.

The middle of the 'A' section provides some contrast by:

➢ Being more contrapuntal in texture – the viola leads off at bar 31 and is imitated a bar later by the cello

➢ Exploring a higher register, especially in the first violin and cello parts

➢ Using more chromatic harmony – indeed, many of the individual parts move by semitone, e.g. the rising first violin part in bars 31–36 and the falling cello part in the same passage

➢ Building to a climax in bar 49 with octave doublings of melodic lines (first violin and viola bar 49–55; first and second violins bar 55–56)

The Trio section from bar 102 is in A major; just as the Scherzo is in the key (D♭), a major 3rd below the key of the first movement (F), so the Trio is in A, a major 3rd below the enharmonic equivalent of D♭, the key of the Scherzo. The Trio is more regular in metre, being in 3/4 and suggesting something of the character of a waltz. Like the 'A' section the downbeat is empty save for the melody; the accompaniment at first is pizzicato. The melody is presented first on the first violin, sul G (on the G string), before the second violin takes over at bar 110, allowing the first violin to play a sighing figure above. From bar 118 the two violins are in dialogue until the main melody returns in the first violin at bar 134, an octave higher than before.

Here the second violin plays a countermelody of detached quavers. The Trio takes on something of the Scherzo character from around bar 149, ready for the return of the A section at bar 159.

There is a seamless link to the coda from around bar 259. Much of the coda is concerned with alternating between the tonic chord of D♭ and the chord on the flattened 6th (variously 'spelled' as A or B♭♭), thereby mirroring the fundamental key relationship of the movement's ternary structure. Tchaikovsky confidently utilises various double-, triple-, and even quadruple-stoppings towards the end.

Dvořák: Piano Quintet in A Op. 81, second movement – Dumka

Antonín Dvořák was one of the most prolific composers in the second half of the 19th century, and he wrote a substantial quantity of chamber music. Czech by birth, he captured many musical traits of his homeland in his musical style, yet gained international standing. It is significant that although the Op. 81 Piano Quintet was written in 1887 following various trips to England, he still wrote a very Czech slow movement in the quintet, called a 'Dumka'.

A dumka is a type of folk music from the Ukraine that was known through the Slavonic world in the 19th century, especially in Bohemia (today's Czech Republic). It originated as a song of lament and later became a slow instrumental piece with a melancholy character, although often there are more cheerful sections interspersed along the way. The dumka is usually in duple time.

The folk origin of the dumka lends a Slavonic flavour to the music and this appealed greatly to Dvořák who regularly turned to this style of piece. Both the String Sextet in A Op. 48 and the String Quartet in E♭ Op. 51 have a dumka as their slow movement and, in particular, the Piano Trio Op. 90 is a unique collection of six movements, each one a dumka, known by the plural of the term as the 'Dumky Trio'.

This second movement of the Piano Quintet is cast in sonata rondo form, a hybrid of sonata and rondo forms usually denoted as ABACABA. The main sections occur as follows:

Bars 1–42	Exposition	A – first subject	F♯ minor	Andante
Bars 43–88		B – second subject	D major	Più mosso
Bars 89–126		A – first subject	F♯ minor	Tempo I
Bars 127–190	Development	C – using motif from bar 3 and triplets from bar 2	various	Vivace
Bars 191–219	Recapitulation	A – first subject	F♯ minor	Tempo I
Bars 220–264		B – second subject	F♯ major	Più mosso
Bars 265–292		A – first subject	F♯ minor	Tempo I
Bars 293–324	Coda	Based on A	F♯ minor	Tempo I

This scheme is similar to sonata form insofar as the second subject is in a related major key in the exposition and then in the tonic major in the recapitulation. Also, the middle section is more tonally unstable, visiting some keys with a remote relationship to the tonic F♯ minor, and making some development of material presented earlier. It is unlike sonata form because of the return to the tonic at the end of the exposition for another statement of the first subject. In this it follows the shape of the rondo, but is unlike rondo in having the 'B' section returning later on (and the way the key scheme effects this section on its two appearances).

The 'A' section comes in two sections, the second of which is repeated. The first (bars 1–15) is framed by a four-bar phrase for solo piano. In between, the main theme is presented on the viola in its rich, low register. Dvořák himself played the viola and this is a fine tune for the instrument; largely conjunct with several semitones and a narrow compass, it has the character of a traditional lament.

The other strings provide a simple chordal accompaniment, although the rich colour of the Neapolitan 6th chord in bar 11 is a moment to savour. Meanwhile a curious countermelody is heard on the piano in octaves in the treble register above the strings.

The second half of the 'A' section continues with a similar texture. Bars 16–19 move towards E minor, but bars 20–23 brings the music back to F♯ minor, whereupon the viola theme from bar 5 appears in the first violin played sul G. The section ends with a reprise of the four-bar piano solo that began the movement. Bars 36–42 form a link to the faster 'B' section.

Folk music is to the fore in the 'B' section. The left hand of the piano provides a decorated drone (suggesting bagpipes – a standard rural folk instrument) and the pizzicato pattern in the viola and cello conjure up an image of village mandolin or dulcimer players. The many cross rhythms – offbeat duplets and triplets in the piano, semiquavers in the viola and cello, and mostly triplets in the melodic material in the violins – also suggest a rustic style of music-making.

The 'B' section follows a similar format to the 'A' section: two halves of which the second is repeated and more diverse tonally. The melodic material moves into the piano in the second half. The key moves towards G minor, then B♭ major and B♭ minor; the melody too is more chromatic with the semitones either side of the dominant note (whichever key the music is in at the time) featuring strongly.

The second 'A' section follows the first closely, but with a complete rescoring.

The development or 'C' section is at a faster tempo. It explores some of the 'A' section material and has a more contrapuntal texture at first, which almost suggests a fugal passage. The music is quite unstable tonally: especially when two bars based on C (bars 139–140) are followed by two based on F♯. The second half of this section takes on the character of a Slavonic dance (of which Dvořák wrote many) and becomes quite frenzied. At bar 185 the piano alone plays a modified version of the opening of the 'C' section at a slower tempo as a link back to F♯ minor and the recapitulation.

In the recapitulation the 'A' section (its third appearance up to this point) is again re-scored and there are harp-like falling arpeggios in the piano accompaniment. The return of the 'B' section is essentially the same as before, other than the change of key. The final appearance of the 'A' section is very like the first, except that it is extended in the beautiful and wistful coda.

Debussy: String Quartet in G minor, second movement – Scherzo

Debussy's String Quartet of 1893 is a pivotal work in the genre and you will immediately hear a more modern approach to quartet writing in this movement than in the other works discussed above. Inspired by the D minor quartet by César Franck of 1889, Debussy's work in turn inspired Ravel to write his quartet in 1903 and had a long-lasting influence on the quartet of the 20th century.

Following Franck's example, Debussy used many thematic connections between movements. Thus much of the material in the Scherzo is derived from the opening bars of the whole quartet:

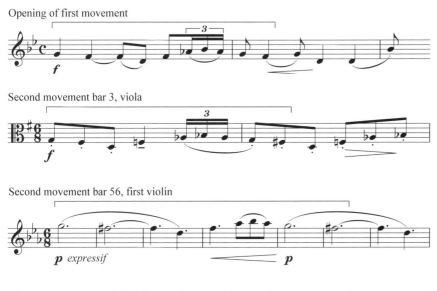

The movement falls into six sections without any clear sense of Classical form, throughout Debussy makes substantial use of pizzicato.

The first section (bars 1–53) is based around G as a tonic, though the liberal use of accidentals undermines any sense of major tonality. After two bars of multi-stop pizzicato chords from first violin and cello, the viola presents the main melodic idea: a version of the opening theme of the first movement. All instruments other than the viola are pizzicato until the first violin takes the melody at bar 37 (by which point the viola is pizzicato).

Duplet quavers add to the rhythmic vitality of the movement, and there are many chromatic inflections both in the melodic material and harmonically; A♭ occurs quite often, sometimes in triple-stopped F minor chords in the cello. From bar 47 the melody is in the cello, and, as it becomes more distant, the upper parts become silent. The cello descends to E♭ at the change of key (to E♭) at fig. 8.

The second section quickly builds an accompanying texture of pizzicato cello alternating between E♭ and B♭ in quavers (in a pattern that cuts across the compound metre) and twitching bowed semiquavers in the viola and second violin. Over this the first violin plays a version of the initial viola theme, now elongated in a much slower rhythm to make a lyrical phrase.

This is an extraordinarily nimble twist of harmonic technique from Debussy, for, despite the change of tonic and key signature, the theme is at the same pitch (if different octave). Initially – in bar 3 – it started on G when this was the tonic; now (bar 56) it begins on G when this is the mediant. Later in this section, at bar 70, the theme starts once more on G when the sense of tonic has moved again, this time to C.

The third section reverts to music more like the opening passage: the main theme is once more in the viola in a more rapid rhythm; however, another, new, melodic strand is simultaneously heard in the cello, and the dynamic markings give this precedence. Duplet quavers again undermine the sense of compound time.

With the music still in a key signature of three flats, the fourth section starts at bar 108 in similar vein to the second section; however, new melodic material is heard in the first violin, played on the G-string. The quadruple semiquavers involved create further cross-rhythms.

A change of key signature at bar 124 marks the start of the fifth section where another version of the main theme is played by the first violin, this time starting on A. Semiquavers in the middle parts and alternating quavers in the cello provide an accompaniment similar to the second section. There is a short linking passage from bar 140 that involves a little antiphony between the two violins and the viola and cello.

The final section is the most unusual of the movement: the music changes into $\frac{15}{8}$ time (five compound beats per bar) and all four instruments are, at first, pizzicato with various multi-stoppings. A new melodic idea on the cello from bar 156 uses many notes from a whole-tone scale, and trills become a strong feature. In a short codetta, the oscillating semiquavers refer back to the second section of the movement.

This movement of 1893 is stylistically far on from the other scherzos we have examined. Debussy shows greater freedom from the magnetism of a tonal centre, from the strictness of regular metrical rhythm, from the blueprint of a particular form, and from the assumption that quartet writing should be primarily dependent on the timbre of bowed string instruments. In all these ways Debussy is pointing towards the new ideas that the 20th century was about to explore.

Area of Study 3c

Four decades of jazz and blues: 1910 to 1950

We know relatively little about popular music before the middle of the 19th century, as it was seldom written down. After about 1850, increasing prosperity led to a demand for new songs that were promoted in the variety shows and music halls of the day. The advent of affordable pianos and cheap music printing led to a market for printed copies of such songs to perform at home, and so popular music regularly appeared in print for the first time.

Much 19th-century popular music was not greatly different from the waltzes, marches and other types of lighter classical music of the period. However, in America the abolition of slavery resulted in excitingly fresh musical ideas coming to public attention as black-American music became more widely known. These included features such as complex syncopation and blue notes (the partially flattened third, fifth and seventh degrees of the major scale) that had originally come from Africa several generations earlier via the slave trade.

By the 1890s, ragtime was the rage – a blend of syncopated rhythms ('ragged time') and familiar western harmonies. The mournful style of the blues took longer to catch on – it was rather too closely identified with black music to be commercially successful at first. However, the invention of the gramophone record led to the rapid spread of all the latest types of popular music in the early 20th century, and an even greater impact resulted from the start of public radio broadcasting in 1920.

By 1920, ragtime was almost forgotten and jazz had become a driving force in much popular music. Unlike ragtime, jazz is not a style of music but a style of performance. In its most common form jazz consists of mainly improvised variations on a chord pattern and so has proved adaptable to changing tastes for almost a century, sometimes being one of the main types of popular music of the day, even influencing composers writing for the concert hall, and at other times being a more specialist type of music, albeit one with a continuing and enthusiastic following.

Resources

For a comprehensive history of jazz, a highly recommended book is *A New History of Jazz* by Alyn Shipton (ISBN: 978-0826447548, Continuum 2007). There are countless recordings which you might like to seek out and collect, but a very useful 2CD anthology is *A History of Jazz from Basin Street to Bebop* (Primo PRMCD6057, 2007).

The specification details certain subsections of this Area of Study which you need to cover. These are:

➢ The blues

➢ Swing music

➢ Big band music

> Bebop

> Orchestral music influenced by jazz and blues.

There are countless pieces from which you could choose. This study guide will focus on a representative sample.

The blues

A jazz standard is a melody that is widely known and held in high regard by jazz musicians as part of their inherited musical repertoire, leading to many versions by different artists.

The blues is one of the most important styles in the early days of the jazz tradition and originated in the southern United States, where it flourished in rural areas among the oppressed immigrant people with African origins. W.C. Handy (1873–1958) was one of the first musicians to notate the now familiar 12-bar blues music in numbers such as *The Memphis Blues* (1912) and *St Louis Blues* (1914), which became 'standards' for many jazz musicians and bands over the following decades.

Handy's style of the blues captured many aspects that became regular features: a 12-bar structure in which the opening four bars of lyrics are repeated before a different final line; a speech-like rhythm to the melodic line and flattened inflections of the major scale in the tune (especially the third, fifth and seventh degrees); and a harmonic pattern across the 12 bars that initially moves from tonic to subdominant, and often consists of the following progression:

Bar 1	Bar 2	Bar 3	Bar 4	Bar 5	Bar 6	Bar 7	Bar 8	Bar 9	Bar 10	Bar 11	Bar 12
I	I	I	I	IV	IV	I	I	V	V	I	I

With all these primary triads being major chords, the flattened notes in the melody sound especially expressive in an often rather mournful manner.

A number of variants of the basic 12-bar chord pattern became common:

> Bar 2: is sometimes chord IV in a version known as 'quick-change' blues

> Bar 10: this is frequently chord IV instead of chord V

> Bar 12: Sometimes this will be chord V instead of chord I to lead back to a repeat of the melody; this feature is known as a 'turnaround'

> Any of the chords (and particularly I in bar 4) may include a minor 7th.

Jelly Roll Morton: Sidewalk Blues (1926)

Ragtime pianist and bandleader Jelly Roll Morton is described by some as the first important jazz composer. Born in 1890 in New Orleans – the first city to embrace the new jazz style – he was playing the piano in the city's bordellos by the age of 12. As early as 1904 he began to travel to many of the southern states, including Memphis, Detroit, St Louis and Kansas City, settling in Los Angeles for five years from 1917. In 1922 he moved to the new hub of the jazz world: Chicago. Here he had his most notable success, making his first recordings and leading a seven- or eight-piece band called the Red Hot Peppers. The 1930s were less successful for him, and he drifted into obscurity. He died in 1941.

Sidewalk Blues captures many of the features of Morton's pioneering jazz style. The instrumentation is that of the 'Dixieland' bands that dominated the New Orleans jazz scene in the early years of the century. There are three 'frontline' instruments – trumpet, trombone and clarinet – which weave polyphonic lines, often improvised, over a 'rhythm section' comprising piano, banjo, and tuba (or string bass).

The number is in a brisk tempo and four beats in a bar; the rhythms are in 'swing' or 'shuffle' style in which notes written as even quavers are played in pairs as long-short, and there are several syncopations where the short note is tied onto the longer note so that the change of note anticipates the beat. There is a succinct introduction in which the three melodic instruments each play an unaccompanied two-bar phrase (there are very short jabbed chords on the downbeats) in the order trombone, trumpet, clarinet, and the final bar of the intro has a very idiomatic high trill on the clarinet (on the dominant).

> Early jazz was not played from sheet music. When you see notated examples remember that they have been transcribed from recordings and so the details of the notation can vary in different editions.

The main melody is then presented on the trumpet:

Points worth listening for are:

➢ Use of syncopations and 'blue' notes in the melody

➢ The repetition of the opening two-bar phrase (but with an altered final note) and the use of the first four notes transposed up a 4th for the next phrase when the chord changes to chord IV.

➢ The staccato chords in the rest of the band that are displaced onto the second and fourth beats of each bar.

➢ The changes to the standard blues chord progression ('chord substitutions') with the bass moving down stepwise halfway through bar 7 to lead to a C major chord in bar 8; this acts as a secondary dominant to chord II (F minor) at the start of the final phrase. The full chord pattern here is:

Bar 1	Bar 2	Bar 3	Bar 4	Bar 5	Bar 6	Bar 7	Bar 8	Bar 9	Bar 10	Bar 11	Bar 12
I	I	I	I^7	IV	IV	I	VI (maj)	II	V	I	I

➢ After some improvisatory development of this first theme, the second half of the number moves to the subdominant key and is more lyrical in nature with some longer, sustained notes in the melodic lines.

Louis Armstrong: West End Blues (1928)

Louis Armstrong (1901–1971) was another influential jazz musician to come from New Orleans, and his musical roots were in the Creole music and early 'hot jazz' of that city. As a young teenager he worked hauling coal to Storyville, the red-light district of New Orleans, and here he listened to the bands playing in the dance halls and brothels. Most notable among these musicians was Joe 'King' Oliver. About this time Armstrong began to play the cornet, later moving to the trumpet. In 1922 Oliver invited Armstrong to join his new jazz band in Chicago; here Armstrong came to fame as a virtuoso trumpeter and soon had his own group, the 'Hot Five'. This group followed a similar format to Jelly Roll Morton's: three melody instruments (trumpet, trombone and clarinet) and a rhythm section comprising piano and banjo.

West End Blues was written by Joe 'King' Oliver, the title referring to a summer weekend resort on Lake Pontchartrain in New Orleans, but it is the recording by Armstrong and his Hot Five that is most famous. The piece is at a lazy, sauntering tempo, and the melody has a mellifluous quality with the initial semitone given prominence:

The chord pattern mainly follows the simple 12-bar blues formula given above.

Armstrong's version is renowned for his remarkable trumpet playing, especially the unaccompanied improvised cadenza with which it starts. There follows five changes of the blues, each featuring a different instrument:

First chorus	Second chorus	Third chorus	Fourth chorus	Fifth chorus
Trumpet	Trombone	Clarinet	Piano	All instruments

Listen out for the following details:

➢ In the first chorus: the use of glissandos in the trombone

➢ In the second chorus: a tremolo effect on the banjo

➢ In the third chorus: Armstrong imitating the clarinet melody (heard in its low chalumeau register) with some relaxed 'scat' (wordless) singing, something for which he was renowned

➢ In the fourth chorus: the varied rhythms and registers in Earl Hines' piano solo

➢ In the fifth chorus: the initial long-held top B♭ on the trumpet; the way the piano is left to play bars 9–12 with the other instruments, re-joining for a brief codetta.

Swing music

As the scope of jazz broadened in the 1920s, so the bands grew in size. Notable bands in the early 1930s included Duke Ellington's band, McKinney's Cotton Pickers and The Casa Loma Orchestra; the first two were 'black bands', but the latter was a 'white band', evidence of the ability of the new music to bridge the huge racial divide in American society.

Typically these bands would have about a dozen musicians: three trumpets, two trombones, three 'reeds' (the term given to a musician doubling saxophone and clarinet), and four in the rhythm section. The tuba of the Dixieland band had now given way to a string bass, and the banjo had been replaced by a guitar. Arrangements would make use of playing the reeds off against the brass (listen to Henderson's *New King Porter Stomp* of 1932) and would often employ short repeating shapes (riffs) taken from the melodic line to accompany instrumental solos, as in *Casa Loma Stomp* (1930).

These techniques made for light and graceful textures that allow for a sense of slick rhythmic momentum and verve, which brings an infectious, toe-tapping quality to the sound. The name given to this quality was 'swing', and it soon became the defining feature of jazz in the 1930s, such that the 'jazz' and 'swing' became interchangeable for a time.

Benny Goodman: Stompin' at the Savoy (1936)

Benny Goodman (1909–1986) is a figure of major significance in the development of swing music. He was born in Chicago, one of 12 children to Jewish parents of Russian descent, and soon came to prominence as a teenage prodigy. His training was broad, including tuition from a classical musician, the influence of playing for a synagogue's boys' band, and the Jewish klezmer style of music. His career blossomed so fast that he soon left school and was touring America with Ben Pollack's band, a 'white band' that was taking jazz to audiences in Los Angeles and New York. He also played on Broadway for Gershwin's *Strike up the Band*.

In 1934 Goodman formed his own band and started to make recordings. Among the band's first numbers was Benny Carter's *Take My Word* in which the four saxophones play melodic lines as four-note chords in parallel motion, a feature that became very idiomatic in swing music. Goodman soon employed Fletcher Henderson who had made an impact with an arrangement of Jelly Roll Morton's *King Porter Stomp*. The band's reputation grew through playing on NBC's Saturday night radio show 'Let's Dance'; by May 1935, when the show went off air, Goodman had over 70 arrangements from Fletcher Henderson. As bands became larger in the swing era, written arrangements became essential, although they usually included sections in which a soloist could improvise over an accompaniment from the rhythm section.

The climax to this period of development was a concert at the Palomar Ballroom in Los Angeles on 21 August 1935 when, after a lukewarm response to various stock arrangements, the audience went wild when the Henderson 'swing' numbers were played. This concert is often seen as the start of the 'swing era'. A famous concert at New York's Carnegie Hall followed in January 1938: all of America was now identifying with jazz. Goodman's career continued to be outstanding, not least in his work with major classical composers including Bartók and Copland.

Stompin' at the Savoy is a jazz standard by Edgar Sampson (the Savoy Ballroom in Harlem, New York operated from 1926–1958 – musically the venue was significant for being home to Chick Webb's band in the mid-1930s, and being where Ella Fitzgerald started her career). The melody is structured in 32-bar song form: there are four eight-bar phrases in which the first, second and last share the same idea and the third brings contrast (AABA). The opening eight-bar phrase starts with a catchy two-bar figure that is repeated in bars 3–4, and adapted for bars 5–6 before a different shape finishes the phrase:

> 32-bar song form was used for many of the slow songs on which jazz standards were based.

Goodman's version is an excellent example of the smooth style of arranging that made his band so popular. There is an efficient four-bar intro and then four choruses of the 32-bar pattern:

➢ **First chorus**: this is the classic 'swing' sound, with the melody in low-register unison saxophones over regular crotchets in the rhythm section. Muted trumpets enter on the third beat of each even-numbered bar – while the saxes hold the long note – and then change chord in anticipation of the next downbeat to emphasise the swing rhythm. The 'B' phrase is similar with slightly more active trumpets.

➢ **Second chorus**: the saxophones lead again, though their melody is now reduced to two notes for each phrase (the first on beat three of the first bar), thereby allowing for a more elaborate response from the trumpets. There is some attractive dynamic shading here. Benny Goodman plays a clarinet solo for the 'B' section over a saxophone accompaniment.

➢ **Third chorus**: this features a slick trombone solo over a saxophone layer and a little more energy and colour from the rhythm section. A tenor sax takes the solo for the B phrase with just the rhythm section for company, before the trombone returns for the last phrase in a slightly more flamboyant mood, using a higher register.

> In a jazz chord substitution, a simple chord is replaced with a more complex chord that has a similar function (e.g. C^7 might be replaced by $Edim^7$).

➢ **Fourth chorus**: now the trumpets come to the fore and there is a 'feel-good' key change up a semitone as they take the melody for the final time. There is some chord substitution deployed. The 'B' section is a second clarinet solo from Goodman: enjoy his sweet, mellifluous tone here. The number ends very efficiently, with Goodman's clarinet having the last two notes.

Big band music

As the popularity of swing music soared, aided by its ability to bring cheer to a country recovering from the Great Depression, so bands began to increase in size and the musical arrangements became more sophisticated. The sax section in particular grew to perhaps five parts (two alto, two tenor and baritone), and having four trumpets and three trombones was now quite common. The drum kit became more prominent in the rhythm section, along with piano, guitar and string bass.

These big bands were also significant in providing musical education to young players. There was little formal education available in jazz until the 1950s, and, in any case, racial discrimination prevented many black musicians from attending conservatoires. Good bandleaders could be dictatorial or more subtle in their management, but their role was not unlike that of a football manager in some senses. Big bands also offered openings for vocalists, both solo singers and backing vocal ensembles.

Count Basie: One O' Clock Jump (1937)

William 'Count' Basie (1904–1984) was born in New Jersey and, after showing an early interest in the drums, became a jazz pianist, playing for the early silent movies as a boy. Travelling in the 1920s he spent some time playing in Harlem and then other important jazz cities including New Orleans, St Louis and Chicago. He met various jazz greats in this time, including Louis Armstrong, before joining one of the first big bands – Walter Page and his Famous Blue Devils – in Tulsa in 1928.

The following year Basie moved on again, this time to Kansas City, and it was here in due course that he founded his own band along with tenor sax player Lester Young. They would regularly play all night for dancers at the Reno Club, often improvising their material over blues patterns. One of these improvisations led to *One O' Clock Jump*, which became the band's signature tune.

The piece is played at a brisk tempo and starts with a section for piano solo (Basie himself) accompanied by drums. Initially a repeating figure in the bass shows more than a hint of boogie-woogie with its rapid swung quavers and chromatic inflection:

The then piano takes the first two blues choruses. This is a quick-change blues in F (i.e. the second bar is chord IV, not chord I). Note the regular crotchets in the rhythm section. At the end of the second time through the blues pattern there are a few tweaks to the chords: listen for the F♯ in the bass of the eighth bar and the way it leads to a G minor chord (chord ii) in the ninth bar; then in the final bar of the pattern the music takes a change of key with a move to D♭ for the next chorus when the rest of the band start playing.

There are a further eight 12-bar choruses that give each member of the band a chance to star (and be introduced to the audience). Enjoy the various solos – especially Lester Young's tenor sax – but listen too for the subsidiary accompanying patterns on other complementary timbres, in order to appreciate how they are built from short repeating figures (like riffs). The full sequence of the piece is:

Section	Intro	1	2	3	4	5	6	7	8	9	10
Key	F	F	F	D♭	D♭	D♭	D♭	D♭	D♭	D♭	D♭
Solo	pno	pno	pno	sax	tmb	sax	tpt	pno	tutti	tutti	tutti
Accompaniment				muted tpt	saxes	muted tpt	tmb	walking str bass			

Duke Ellington: Take the 'A' Train (1941)

Born in Washington in 1899, Duke Ellington is one of the most influential figures in the history of jazz, whose work was as versatile as it is significant. He made his professional debut as a pianist at the age of 17 and moved to New York in 1923 with a band called the Washingtonians. Over the next five years this band, which played at clubs on Broadway, grew to be ten strong. When, in 1927, Joe 'King' Oliver turned down an invitation to become the house band at the Cotton Club – a famous nightclub in the heart of Harlem – Duke Ellington was given the position. Here, over the next five years, he developed the band and musical style that made his reputation.

The period from 1932–1942 was Ellington's most creative. His band now comprised 14 musicians (six brass, four reeds and four in the rhythm section) and he took them on several tours around America and twice to Europe. In the Cotton Club itself, Ellington not only was responsible for the dance tunes but also the overtures and other music for the shows. This gave him the freedom to experiment with orchestral colours and special effects that other bands seldom enjoyed.

He had a very refined aural imagination and created unusual scorings that gave his band a distinctive sound. The standard New Orleans texture would have the clarinet in a high register with an obbligato line, the trumpet in mid-register with the main theme, and the trombone below with a counter-melody; however, in Ellington's big hit *Mood Indigo* (1930) the muted trumpet is heard on top, the trombone with plunger-mute provides a second high-register voice, and the clarinet in its chalumeau register sounds more than an octave lower.

As Ellington's work became more explorative, so it came to rely more on composition than improvisation. In particular, he experimented with structure: for instance in *Concerto for Cootie* (1940) he built a ternary form from ten-bar phrases. *Black, Brown and Beige*, a work written for a Carnegie Hall concert in 1943 and intended to tell the history of black people in the USA, uses almost symphonic techniques in its manipulation of motivic material. After the Second World War he wrote film scores and sacred music, notably *In the Beginning God* (1965). Ellington died in 1974.

Take the 'A' Train refers to the subway line that ran from New York City to the jazz territory of Harlem. The song was written by Billy Strayhorn, whom Ellington employed as a composer and also second pianist for the band. It soon became the band's signature tune in the 1940s.

There is a brief piano intro that alternates between the tonic chord in second inversion and a chromatic chord built on F♯; the melodic fragment used here is a fragment of a descending whole-tone scale. The main tune follows the standard 32-bar song form (AABA). The melody is heard first on unison saxes. The main rhythmic interest in the theme is in the second bar: elsewhere it depends on long notes that allow for rhythmic interjections from other sections of the band, such as the trumpets and trombones. These contribute chord stabs at different times during the first two eight-bar phrases.

In the 'B' phrase the trumpets are silent, but the trombones continue to insert chords under the melody's long notes; in the final 'A' phrase trumpets return, but now play with the trombones for a more full brass sound.

The second time through the melody is on a muted trumpet and the saxes provide a soft, velvety backdrop with some beautiful sustained playing. For the third and final time through the tune, the key moves up a 3rd to E major; the saxophones take the main melodic material, though a flamboyant solo trumpet (unmuted now) draws the listener's attention rather more. Some of the chords are now quite dissonant, giving both an echo of train hooters and a hint of a more modern harmonic palette that jazz was to take over the next couple of decades. The second half of the verse gradually fades and the number ends with soft, low sax tones.

Bebop

During the 1940s, a new generation of jazz musicians were coming to the fore and wanting to make a mark. Some took a retrospective view and returned to the origins of the style in New Orleans. Meanwhile, others based in New York searched for a modern jazz idiom. Among these were Kenny Clarke (drums), Dizzy Gillespie (trumpet), Thelonious Monk (piano), Charlie Parker (saxophone), Bud Powell (piano) and Max Roach (drums).

These prodigious young musicians would experiment in their after-hours 'jam sessions' in Harlem's small nightclubs (most notably 'Minton's Playhouse'), and they developed new ideas on harmonic substitutions, rhythmic vocabulary and melodic construction. Gillespie later said: 'On afternoons before a session, Thelonious Monk and I began to work out some complex variations on chords and the like, and we used them at night to scare away the no-talent guys'. Similarly, Parker recalled an occasion when 'I was working over *Cherokee* and, as I did, I found that by using the higher intervals of a chord as a melody line and backing them with related changes, I could play the thing I'd been hearing'.

Among the harmonic tricks these musicians used was making chromatic alterations to various degrees of diatonic chords: flattened 5th and 9th, sharpened 9th, or flattened 13th. Meanwhile, melodic phrasing gradually became more asymmetric and less regular, so that phrases would be independent of the patterns inherent in the harmonic progressions (i.e. where the cadences occur), as can be heard in Charlie Parker's solos in *Moten Swing* (1940).

The rhythmic language became more complex in its syncopations; unlike swing which emphasised the natural strong beats (beats 1 and 3), now the backbeats (2 and 4) became stressed, creating a greater sense of rhythmic propulsion. Drummers, led by Clarke, now used the hi-hat or ride cymbal for a regular time-keeping pattern, freeing the bass drum (which had traditionally done this task in swing music) to play accents known as 'dropping bombs'. One other implication was that the bass line became more important, both for underpinning the more advanced harmonic palette and for keeping time: the string bass now is very active in playing fast-moving 'walking bass' lines.

Dizzy Gillespie: Groovin' High (1945)

Gillespie was born in a rural farming community in South Carolina in 1917, the youngest child of a bricklayer-cum-bandleader. He taught himself to play various brass instruments and also learned piano. Gillespie's early career took him to Philadelphia and then, in 1937, to New York where he played with Teddy Hall's big band.

On tour in 1940 to Kansas City he met Charlie Parker and back in New York they began to collaborate on the development of the new bebop style. They found their ideas had developed independently along very similar tracks and in due course they played together in various small jazz ensembles.

Groovin' High is a Gillespie composition based on a chord sequence from a 1920 jazz standard called *Whispering* by John Schonberger. It was one of seven tracks released on the album *Shaw 'Nuff* that made a big impact on Gillespie's contemporaries. Though less than 3 minutes long, this track shows many aspects of the detail Gillespie brought to his musical style.

The piece starts with a carefully composed introduction in which the saxophones are in dialogue with the string bass which, briefly, is bowed. There are some subtle effects on the drums too. Similarly the falling 3rd motif at the start of the melody is imitated on the piano. Throughout this section the brushes on the snare and the pizzicato walking bass maintain the rhythmic momentum. Listen for the colourful circle of 5ths chords just after the 0'45" point at the end of the first main section.

The middle break returns to using the bowed string bass; shortly afterwards Gillespie enters with a scintillating virtuoso trumpet solo with very fluid rhythmic character and free sense of phrase-length. He then also makes use of a brief guitar solo. The coda, where Gillespie again shines, is at half tempo.

Orchestral music influenced by jazz and blues

The history outlined in this section from the blues to bebop indicates how quick American musicians were to find potential in the new field of jazz. Such was the growth in its profile over this period that it was only a matter of time before its influence was felt in the concert hall. That it should be an American composer who first found ways to explore a 'crossover' approach is no surprise. George Gershwin (1898–1937) blended classical and jazz elements in a highly successful career cut short by a brain tumour. Gershwin's main area of activity was in writing shows for Broadway, and his musical language was ideally suited to the task. Gershwin also tried his hand at concert works and it is here that the musical syntax of the new jazz meets the world of the symphony orchestra. The two most successful works that you should look at are his highly popular *Rhapsody in Blue* (1924) with its instantly memorable opening of the clarinet glissando, and the lesser-known Piano Concerto in F of the following year.

If it is almost to be expected to find an American composer exploring the fusion of jazz and classical elements, it is rather more surprising that before the 1920s were out a French composer was showing an interest in jazz. In 1929 Ravel began his Piano Concerto in G, which shows many influences of the new jazz style, especially in its outer movements with a rhythmic zest and flamboyant use of colour. An even greater shock is to find Shostakovich in Soviet Russia writing two jazz suites in the 1930s (No. 1, 1934; No. 2, 1938). Jazz tended to be considered a decadent, bourgeois form of western culture and only some filtered through. Shostakovich's suites are more in a light classical style than real jazz, but give him a chance to display his skill for brilliant and witty orchestration.

Unit 5: Developing Musical Ideas

This is a coursework unit with a very similar structure to Unit 2, which you will have done as part of your AS course. AQA will issue the 'briefs' paper on 1 November. At some point after that date you will start 20 hours of supervised time during which you will complete the work to be submitted. This will need to be complete soon after the start of May for your work to be sent to an AQA examiner.

It is likely that you will decide to take the equivalent option on this paper that you chose for Unit 2 in your AS course, but there is no obligation to do this. Perhaps, if you were a little disappointed with your mark at Unit 2, it might be worth considering a different option this time. Even if you were pleased with your Unit 2 mark, you might like a change at A2 to broaden the experience you gain from A level music.

The three briefs set by AQA are:

➤ Compositional techniques: completing two set exercises

➤ Free composition or pastiche: writing a 5- to 8-minute long piece

➤ Arranging: making an arrangement of a set piece of popular 'classical' music that puts the original piece into a pop, rock or jazz style.

Advice on how to complete Brief A follows below. If you are choosing one of the other options, turn to page 126 for Brief B or page 129 for Brief C.

Note that the work you submit has to be completed at your school or college – you are not allowed to take it home, or to submit material that has been downloaded from the internet. You should have plenty of time before starting on your chosen brief to learn and practise the relevant techniques.

Brief A: Compositional techniques

Outline

You have to complete two tasks for Brief A:

➤ Question 1: harmonisation of a Bach chorale melody

➤ Question 2: the Classical string quartet.

Harmonisation of a Bach chorale melody

You will be given a melody (soprano part) of the type that is found in the Lutheran tradition of hymns, otherwise known as chorales. Your task is to add parts for alto, tenor and bass, following in the style of J. S. Bach.

In many ways this is a similar task to Question 1 from Brief A in Unit 2, which you may have done for your AS. You may like

Each task is marked out of 30, so they have equal weight. Bear this in mind when you are working at the questions in the supervised time, and do not become so obsessed with seeking the perfect solution for one that you do not leave enough time to write a good answer for the other.

to remind yourself of the basics of choosing appropriate chords, composing cadences and creating good part-writing that were covered in Rhinegold Education's AS Music Study Guide for AQA (see pages 93–97), and this would be a very good place to start if you are new to this topic, having tried Brief B or C for Unit 2.

The main questions to ask yourself when completing this exercise are:

➤ In which key does each phrase cadence? (Reminder: available keys are the tonic, subdominant, dominant and the relative of each of these three keys – a total of six possible keys)

➤ What type of cadence does each phrase require? (Reminder: the majority of cadences in chorales are perfect, and most of the rest are imperfect)

➤ What choice of chords is available for each note of the melody? (Reminder: the note in the tune could be the root, 3rd or 5th of the chord, unless it is a non-chord note)

➤ Does every chord you've written include a root, a 3rd and a 5th? (Reminder: there will probably be two tonics, or possibly two 5ths)

➤ Does the tenor part lie quite high? (Reminder: it should often use leger lines above the bass clef stave)

➤ Does your part writing avoid consecutive 5ths and octaves? (Note: some software packages include a function for checking this automatically).

In addition to these basics of good harmony, the A2 specification lists various features of the Bach chorale style for which the examiners will give particular credit. Several of these are explained in the first section of this book:

➤ Accented passing notes (see below)

➤ Suspensions (see pages 19–20)

➤ Chromatic harmony (see page 13 under 'secondary 7ths')

➤ Diminished 7ths (see page 11)

➤ Third inversion chords (see page 14).

The only way to learn how to complete the harmonisation of a chorale in the style of Bach is to become familiar with original examples found in Bach's choral works. Most of his cantatas finish with a chorale, and there are several in the major choral works such as the Passions and the Christmas Oratorio. These provide the best way of learning about the style. Try playing the chorales at the piano, or find an opportunity to sing some of them, either in a choir or with three other musical friends.

If you are undertaking this brief it may be worth looking at the *AS Music Harmony Workbook* (ISBN: 978-1-906178-34-5) and *A2 Music Harmony Workbook* (ISBN: 978-1-906178-39-0), both written by Hugh Benham and published by Rhinegold Education.

> **Resources**
>
> You may want to obtain a copy of the collected Bach chorales: *Bach – 371 Harmonised Chorales*, edited by Albert Riemenschneider, published by Schirmer.

Stylistic ways of creating quaver motion in your chorale harmony include:

- Passing notes: if one of the lower parts has a small leap of a 3rd, try filling it in with a quaver passing note on the half-beat; alternatively try putting the passing note on the second beat, and then delay the harmony note of the second chord by half a beat to create an accented passing note.

- Suspensions: if an inner part is moving downwards by conjunct motion, try holding on to the first note for half a beat longer and see if it produces that idiomatic moment of dissonance that can then resolve downwards on the half beat.

- Changing from root position to first inversion: this will give you a consonant option for quaver movement in the bass line.

Stylistic writing

Below are two examples of four-part harmonisations by Bach. Each example is followed by a short analysis of the key features used within the harmonisation, which are strongly typical of the idiom. In addition to the specific points mentioned, consider the following aspects in each chorale:

➤ What range of keys is used for the cadences?

➤ Which of the three harmony parts (A, T or B) has the most leaps? (Try playing or singing each part in turn.)

➤ Which part most often requires leger lines?

➤ How many crotchet beats includes a pair of quavers in at least one of the parts?

➤ How often is the bass part in contrary motion with the melody?

You should aim to make your harmonisation reflect the characteristics that the questions above identify.

Example 1: 'Brich an, o schönes Morgenlicht' from *Christmas Oratorio*, part II, movement 12

Note the following aspects:

➤ Bar 1^3: the C♯ in the melody could be treated as an unaccented passing note, with the alto and tenor having a crotchet on the beat. Instead, Bach doubles the melody a 6th below in the alto part to include an additional passing note. To add further interest, the second half of the beat becomes a new chord by changing the tenor note too. The result is a secondary 7th – V^7 of V – in third inversion (V^7d).

➢ Bar 2^4: the diatonic option would have been chord I (G major) at this point, with the B in the soprano as the 3rd. Instead Bach sees the opportunity for chromaticism, and uses a secondary 7th – this time V^7 of VI – in first inversion. As a further elaboration, the secondary 7th does not lead to an expected E minor chord at the beginning of bar 3, but instead goes to C major in first inversion – almost like an interrupted cadence progression.

➢ Bar 3: this is the first bar (but not the last) in which the bass part has quavers throughout the bar. Most interesting is the octave leap in the middle onto the third inversion of the dominant 7th (V^7d). Also notice that on the fourth beat of the bar, the harmony note in the bass is the G on the half-beat – the A that is played on the beat is therefore an accented passing note.

➢ Bar 5^2: this beat comes in the middle of a standard Ib–VIIb–I progression, though in A minor just for this phrase (the Ib chord is on the half-beat of 5^1). Bach delays the appearance of the G♯ in the alto by a quaver, thereby benefiting threefold: the beat itself has a 7-6 suspension (A over B); quaver motion is created; attention is drawn to the chromaticism of the G♯ sounding by itself on the half-beat.

➢ Bar 5^4: Bach uses a diminished 7th chord here, which operates as a secondary 7th. It can also be analysed as a B^7 chord (the dominant of the forthcoming E chord), but with the root (B) substituted by a minor 9th (the C in the soprano).

➢ Bar 7: for this phrase in E minor, Bach finds a powerful rising chromatic bass line. It is made possible by the use of two secondary 7ths, both in first inversion: V^7 (E^7) of IV (A minor) on the second beat, and V^7 ($F\sharp^7$) of V (B) on the fourth beat. The second of these is initially a diminished 7th chord due to the quaver G in the alto; both chords pass on to their expected destination.

➢ Bar 9: throughout this penultimate phrase of the chorale, the bass flows in quavers that are mostly conjunct in descent, as a release to the tension caused by the rising chromatic crotchets of the previous phrase. Further tension is created, however, by the interaction of the soprano and alto parts in the second half of the bar, where suspensions on both beats 3 and 4 resolve on the half-beats.

➢ Bar 11: the tenor creates a sequence of suspensions as the chorale moves to its final cadence.

➢ Bar 12^1: Bach saves the only use of semiquavers in the whole chorale for the final cadence pattern. Unusually there is no 7th used in the final dominant chord on beat 2 of the bar.

Example 2: 'O grosse Lieb' from *St John Passion*, part I, movement 7

Note the following aspects:

➢ Bar 1^2: the chord Bach chooses here is first inversion of C minor (IVb), as the first chord in an imperfect cadence. The tenors need a G to complete the chord, which can be approached via an A passing note from the previous B♭. Bach sees the opportunity here of placing the passing note on the beat, thereby creating quaver motion on both beats 1 and 2 of the bar.

➢ Bar 1^4: Bach starts the next phrase using the third inversion of the dominant 7th (V^7d), which proceeds in the standard progression to Ib on the downbeat of the next bar. This creates an effective conjunct bass part that covers six degrees of the scale.

➢ Bar 3^1: Bach could easily have used V^7b here. However, swapping the D for an E♭ in the tenor part creates a diminished 7th chord, which provides a more plangent effect in a minor key context.

➢ Bar 4^4: in this phrase (which ends in the relative major of B♭), Bach uses another dominant 7th in third inversion. However, this time it is a secondary 7th: V7d of IV.

➢ Bar 5^2: this could form a rather static moment of harmony: the repeated E♭ in the melody could lead to two consecutive beats of IVb. Bach skilfully twists this with a chromatic inflection as the bass note slips from G to G♭, and thereby changes chord IV in B♭ major to the equivalent chord in B♭ minor – this is a trick more associated with early Romantic composers.

➢ Bar 5^4: prior to the perfect cadence in B♭ major, Bach uses a secondary 7th again – V^7b of V – though the quaver D♭ in the soprano makes it a diminished 7th chord.

➢ Bar 7^2: another diminished 7th chord that is actually a dominant minor 9th of the following D minor chord – the root (A) having been swapped for the minor 9th (B♭) in the tenor.

➢ Bar 8^{1-2}: two potentially static beats – repeating melody notes with the same chord – are given a stylistic dressing by moving to the first inversion of the chord on the second beat; the change facilitates quaver passing notes in the alto and bass.

Bach maintains the quaver motion in the bass by returning to root position on the half-beat of beat 2.

➤ Bar 8³⁻⁴: a pair of suspensions in the alto – a 9-8 followed by a 7-6 – generates more quaver motion and an idiomatic counterpoint between soprano and alto parts.

➤ Bar 10: this final phrase includes not one but two 'fingerprint' leaps downwards of a diminished 5th in the bass. The first of these (onto beat 1) arrives on a diminished 7th chord; the second (onto beat 3) arrives on a secondary 7th chord – V⁷b of V.

➤ Bar 11: typical of all Bach chorales in minor keys, the final chord is the major version of chord I, otherwise known as a tierce de Picardie.

Exercise 30

Here is a chorale-style melody for you to harmonise:

Once you have completed your own harmonisation of this chorale, have a look at Bach's own version. The original can be found in the *St. John Passion*, part I, movement 9.

The Classical string quartet

You will be given the first-violin part of a section of a Classical string quartet. Your task is to add parts for second violin, viola and cello in the style of a composer such as Haydn.

Although this question requires you to work within the set style, there is more freedom here for how you go about your answer than in a Bach chorale. String instruments have a wider range than choral singers, the harmonic rhythm is unlikely to be rigidly one chord per beat but will fluctuate instead, and there is more scope for being imaginative with the texture. Certainly you do not have to write one note in each of the lower three parts for every note in the given first violin part, and sometimes it may be appropriate to have rests in one or more of the lower parts. It is also possible that the first violin part will have a bar's rest, or just a long sustained note, in which case you may need to compose some melodic material for one of the lower parts.

Otherwise this question calls for a similar understanding of four-part harmony, with convincing harmonic progressions, good cadences and musical part-writing, but cast in a way suitable for string instruments.

If you are a string player, try to play some quartets of this period with a group of friends (if you're a violinist, make sure you have a go at both first and second violin parts). If you do not play a string instrument you might still be able to adapt a part to play on your instrument. Also, spend some time talking to string players so you learn from them about the capabilities of their instrument.

Web link

Scores for Haydn's and Mozart's quartets can be found for free at http://imslp.org/

The only way to learn how to write string quartet music is to listen to and study original examples from the period. The string quartet was essentially Haydn's invention, and his quartets – he wrote at least 68 of them – should be your starting point; you may also like to look at quartets by Mozart.

Stylistic writing

Below are two examples taken from quartet movements by Haydn. Each example is followed by a short analysis of the key features used within the part-writing, which are strongly typical of the idiom. In addition to the specific points mentioned, consider the following aspects in each quartet:

➢ How many rests are used?

➢ How often do two parts move in parallel 3rds or 6ths?

➢ When are pedal notes used and how are they handled?

➢ How clear is it what the role of each part is: melody, countermelody, accompaniment figuration, bass line, etc.?

Example 1: String Quartet in A major No. 2, Op. 20, second movement, bars 1–14

Note the following aspects:

➢ Bars 1–2: a simple I–V–I–V progression, which is made idiomatic through the use of quaver rests and offbeat notes in the second violin and viola, and the chord inversions used to make a bass line in crotchets (I–Ib–V^{7}c–V^7).

➢ Bar 3: the run of semiquavers is left unaccompanied by the lower parts.

➢ Bar 4: a simple imperfect cadence. Note that the harmonic rhythm has so far moved as follows: a change of harmony every two beats (bars 1–2); a bar with only one chord on the downbeat (bar 3); a cadence where the harmony moves in crotchets (bar 4).

➢ Bars 5–6: there is a suggestion of a harmonic sequence here while Haydn maintains the texture established at the outset.

➢ Bars 7^4–8^1: a perfect cadence despite the delayed resolution to the tonic in the first-violin part. Note that (unlike in Bach chorales) the fifth degree of the tonic chord is not used here – this is quite a common feature of the Classical style. Instead there are three roots (E) and a major 3rd (G♭).

➢ Bar 8$^{2-4}$: Haydn finds a simple harmonic formula to link the end of the opening musical sentence (ending on chord I) to the start of the next (also beginning on I): IV–Ib–VIIb.

➢ Bar 9: at the start of the second musical sentence – where the melody is the same as the first – Haydn constructs a more luxurious texture with a semiquaver figuration in the second violins (note the rests on the beats), while the viola and cello work in harmony (note the spacing here). One of the significant factors is the contrast this makes to the opening, simpler texture – a degree of advance planning is required to achieve this stylistic effect.

➢ Bars 11–12: note the use of a tonic pedal in these bars; particularly idiomatic is the use of V^7 over the tonic pedal in bar 12$^{3-4}$.

➢ Bar 13: another bar of semiquaver activity in the first violin, which is left largely unaccompanied by the lower strings.

➢ Bar 14: the imperfect cadence here is of the 'half-close' kind where Ic precedes V. This is a typical Classical period feature.

Example 2: String Quartet in D major No. 6, Op. 50, first movement, bars 1–16

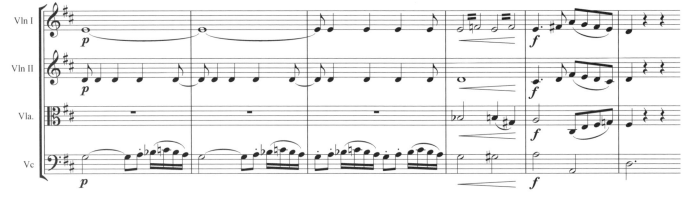

Double-stopping

String instruments are capable of playing more than one note, if the bow is used at the right angle to play two strings simultaneously. Writing in double stops for a string instrument requires an advanced understanding of playing techniques, in order to know which combinations of notes are easy, difficult or impossible to play. If you are not a string player, it may be best to avoid double-stopping; in any case, it was not common in the Classical period. However, 3rds, 4ths and 6ths can be used with confidence, so long as both notes are not in the bottom 4th of the instrument's range – as this would require the lowest string to produce both notes simultaneously.

Note the following aspects:

➤ Bars 2–4: a standard diatonic progression of V⁷b–I–IIb–Ic–V–I; note how fluid the harmonic rhythm is.

➤ Bars 4–7: Haydn uses a tonic pedal, but unlike the previous example, he opts to have static inner parts (including double stops in the second violin). Instead, the tonic pedal is made active through the hopping between octaves.

➤ Bar 8: a semiquaver scale in the first violin is left largely unaccompanied by the lower strings.

➤ Bars 9–10: unusually the viola plays lower than the cello; here the cello is, perhaps, being prepared for its forthcoming melodic line. Note how the second violin fills in when the first violin rests in the second half of the bar, by imitating the first-violin figure from the start of the bar.

➤ Bars 11–12: with the first violin clearly not having the melodic interest here, Haydn writes a tune for the cello and takes the opportunity to pretend the piece is in D minor rather than D major for a few bars. The texture is reduced to three parts. Note how the second violin, although *p*, brings some energy and intensity to the music by reiterating its note on every half-beat (a typical Classical period feature).

➤ Bar 143: the return to the tonic major is prepared by the use of a secondary dominant – V^{7}b of V.

➤ Bar 15: the two violins are in parallel 3rds throughout this bar.

Exercise 31

Here is the first-violin part from a passage of a Haydn string quartet for you to practise part-writing:

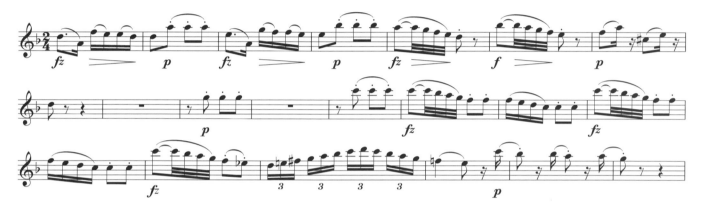

Once you have completed your own part-writing for this passage, have a look at Haydn's own version. The original can be found in his String Quartet in D minor, Op. 42, first movement, bars 1–21.

The review

When you have completed your answers you have to write a review of your work, evaluating the success of the work you are going to submit; this should show awareness of the conventions of the two styles in which you have had to compose. The review may be completed outside the period of 'controlled time'.

Brief B: Free composition or pastiche

Outline

If you choose Brief B your task is to compose one piece of music that lasts between 5 and 8 minutes.

Your piece can be of any genre and use any combination of instruments, voices or electronic sound sources. The piece can be in a single movement, or can comprise up to three separate but related sections or movements.

It is necessary to submit both a recording of your piece and a score or annotation of some kind. If you are reluctant to provide a fully notated score, make sure your annotation has information about how you have controlled all musical elements within your piece, and in particular gives detailed information about the structure of your composition.

Aspects to bear in mind

There are so many elements to a piece of music that it is very easy to overlook some of the aspects for which the examiners will be looking. These will include:

➢ Is there a clear structure to your piece?

➢ Have you explored the potential of your musical ideas through their development?

➢ Are you in control of the tonality of the music?

➢ Does the harmonic language bring character and direction to the music?

➢ Have you clearly imagined the resulting sound of the timbres you have employed and the texture you have created with them?

➢ Is the writing for each instrument idiomatic and well marked up with performance detail?

➢ Are you in overall control of the musical character of your piece?

Be mindful of the mark scheme: credit can be given for your handling of elements such as melody and harmony, so it would be ill-advised to write a piece solely for untuned percussion. The specification also suggests that you should show some grasp of tonality, so think twice before embarking on an atonal project: it would be best at least to blend atonal passages and ideas with having a tonal centre. For instance, perhaps you could write a set of three movements where atonal, whole-tone and serial compositions are related in some way.

Method

It is almost impossible to explain how the composing process starts. Somehow, either in the silence of your inner ear, or through the semi-conscious movement of your fingers in improvising on your instrument, musical ideas will come to you. The most significant thing is what happens after that.

It can be very tempting to keep repeating that first moment time and time again. Your silent musings, or your improvising, tumble ever-onwards, and before long the first idea you had is long-forgotten. If this process goes on unchecked, it is possible to complete an hour of 'composing', for the bell to go / lunch to be served / your mate to knock on your door, etc., and for the session to come to an abrupt end with nothing to show for your labours. By the time you return to composing, perhaps the next day, nothing of your previous session can be re-captured, and you must start again from the beginning. One can soon become very disheartened by the notion of composing.

The problem is that what is described in the paragraph above is not really composing; rather it is the musical equivalent of doodling. Composition certainly involves that slightly mysterious, indefinable process of musical ideas entering your head, but it needs more than this. Composition means becoming fascinated with one particular such idea – capturing it in a permanent form before it evaporates in the onward rush of brain activity – and then working with it, much like a sculptor works with a lump of granite or piece of driftwood, to see what music can be made from the original idea.

It is vitally important, therefore, to force yourself to frequently and regularly make sketches of the ideas you have. This can be done in a very rough, shorthand way: it only has to be enough to jog your memory at this stage. Once the idea can be seen you then have something with which to begin the process of composition. Now you can think through what the potential of your idea is. Try asking the following questions of your idea:

➢ What is its musical character?

➢ What instrument(s) best suit it?

➢ Which register best suits it?

➢ What are its constituent parts?

➢ Which musical elements are most important to it?

➢ What is the best tempo for it?

➢ How suited is the idea to repetition, sequence, inversion, decoration, etc.?

➢ What other material combines well with the original idea?

Pursuing some of the answers to these questions should help you to take your musical idea forwards and soon you will have a sense of where the idea can lead you and what sort of piece you are trying to write.

Plan ahead: you do not have to compose the bars of your piece in chronological order. When will your piece need a second contrasting idea? What sort of contrast will be required? What happens in the middle? How will the piece end? All the while sketch in shorthand the ideas you have for the piece. Sometimes you will want to refine a particular phrase or moment in some detail; at other times it will be important to consider the bigger picture. An artist will often sketch in the outline of a painting before mixing the paint; they will sometimes work at one corner and then move to a different place on the canvas. Your process should be something similar.

As more and more of the piece takes shape, remain analytical about how it is coming together. Sometimes, quite late in the process, you will realise that another instrument is needed, that

Creating contrast

Sooner or later you will need to have a section that brings contrast to your composition; this may be the second movement of a three-movement scheme, or just a new section in a single piece. Consider changing one or more (but probably not all) of the following aspects of your piece as ways to make contrast:

➢ Key
➢ Tempo
➢ Metre
➢ Melodic material
➢ Instrumentation
➢ Dynamic
➢ Texture
➢ Register
➢ Articulation
➢ Phrase lengths
➢ Harmonic rhythm
➢ Rhythmic character
➢ Accompanimental figuration.

a particular section could be developed further, or a new linking passage inserted. Sometimes you will realise that the piece might be better for cutting out a passage.

Managing 'controlled time'

The period of 20 hours in which you have to write your final composition will, in all likelihood, not start until well into the second term of your course. This gives you ample opportunity to experiment with various ideas before then. Although you are not allowed to take any written material into the 'controlled time' period, there is no reason why you cannot commit some of your best ideas to memory and re-create them in the allotted time. This should allow you to arrive at the venue for your 'controlled time' work ready to make the most of the time from the first hour.

Similarly, there is nothing to stop you remembering the work you have done during the 'controlled time' and exploring its potential further outside the official time spent at your exam centre.

Preparing a score

If you are preparing a score to submit to the examiners, remember that a finished score needs to give the following information:

➢ What notes should be played

➢ When they should be played

➢ How they should be played

➢ Who should be playing them.

For advice on preparing an annotation see page 131.

You should therefore give as much detail as possible regarding tempo markings, performance directions and expression markings. Try to avoid excessive leger lines, either by a change of clef where appropriate, or use of the 8va sign. Also make sure you take control of the stave size to create a sensible layout; sometimes the default setting in the software can lead to little more than one bar of score per page: not the easiest layout for the examiner, or indeed yourself, to review the quality of the composition.

The review

When you have completed your composition you have to write a review of your work, evaluating the success of the piece you are going to submit. The review may be completed outside the period of controlled time.

Brief C: Arranging

Outline

In this brief AQA will set a well-known piece of classical music from any period of music history from the Baroque period onwards. Your task is to write an arrangement of the piece in a pop, jazz or rock style that lasts between 5 and 8 minutes.

Whichever style you choose, the ensemble for which you write must include a rhythm section involving drum kit and/or percussion, either double bass or bass guitar, and another guitar and/or a keyboard instrument. Beyond this the choice of instrumentation is up to you and can involve electronic sound sources if you wish.

It is necessary to submit both a recording of your piece and a score or annotation of some kind. If you are reluctant to provide a fully notated score, make sure your annotation has information about how you have controlled all of the musical elements within your piece, and in particular gives detailed information about the structure of your composition.

Aspects to bear in mind

Although everyone choosing to do this brief will be starting from the same set piece, there are many directions in which you could take this task. The following points are important to think about:

➤ You do not have to use all of the given material – perhaps there are two or three main themes on which you wish to base your piece.

➤ You can change any aspect of the piece you wish, for instance the key, tempo or metre, if you think it serves the style you are using for your arrangement.

➤ Your arrangement should have a clear structure, which may be different to the original piece.

➤ It might be effective to change key for various sections of the piece.

➤ You should be in control of the harmonic vocabulary of the piece: perhaps you are basing this closely on the original, but you may prefer a more repetitive pattern, perhaps involving power chords for a rock version, or a more elaborate palette of chords involving 9ths and 13ths for a jazz arrangement.

➤ Think carefully about the sound of the timbres you choose for your arrangement, and the texture you have created with them; try to imagine the resulting sound, and sense the right place in the structure to vary this.

➤ Make sure the writing for each instrument is idiomatic and well-marked up with performance detail.

Method

The set piece that you are using must be central to your arrangement. It is therefore vitally important to become very familiar with it.

If possible, listen to a range of recordings of the piece, and play through as much of it as you can on your own instrument.

Any substantial piece will comprise many different musical ingredients. Try to isolate some in the piece you are arranging that particularly interest you: it might be a melodic shape, a bass line, a chord progression, or some other feature. Experiment with using these in different ways: perhaps change the tempo or metre, or try a different kind of texture. Once you have found a way of giving this aspect of the original piece a particular musical character of your own, you have the basis for a potential first section of your arrangement.

A piece that lasts 5–8 minutes is a substantial one, and this will need some careful planning. It may well be that your first section will return on two or three occasions, and you may wish to keep some extra element to it in reserve for a later appearance: a climactic ostinato high on the lead guitar, a funkier drum pattern, or a more active double-bass part, for instance. Perhaps these can replace the drone that you use for its first appearance. Or maybe it will return in a higher key, with a louder dynamic, at a faster tempo or a different instrumentation (maybe the sax taking the solo rather than the trumpet).

There will also be a point at which you will need some contrasting material. This too should be based on the original set piece, but there are plenty of other ways in which you can make a subsidiary passage create contrast in your arrangement. See page 127 for some ideas on how to create contrasting material.

As more and more of the piece takes shape, remain analytical about how it is coming together. Sometimes, quite late in the process, you will realise that another instrument is needed, that a particular section could be developed further, or a new linking passage inserted. Sometimes you will realise that the piece might be better for cutting out a passage. Above all, try to make sure that the sense of idiom is consistent, and that the original piece is clearly the basis of your work consistently and hasn't been left behind halfway through your arrangement.

Managing 'controlled time'

The period of 20 hours in which you have to write your final arrangement will, in all likelihood, not start until well into the second term of your course. This gives you ample opportunity to experiment with various techniques for arranging music in your preferred style before then. Although you are not allowed to take any written material into the 'controlled time' period, there is no reason why you cannot commit some of your best ideas to memory and make use of them in the allotted time.

Similarly, there is nothing to stop you remembering aspects of the set piece during the first few sessions of 'controlled time' and exploring its potential further outside the official time spent at your exam centre, although you will not be allowed to take any written material with you back into the venue for 'controlled time' work.

Preparing an annotation

If you are thinking of submitting an annotation rather than a score, make sure you spend enough time on this to show as much detail as possible. In particular make sure the following information is clearly visible to the examiner:

➢ The structure of your piece

➢ The main musical material you have used, including chord progressions, melodic shapes and rhythm patterns

➢ Which instruments are required and the role each one takes in each section of the piece

➢ Performance directions such as tempo, dynamics and instrumental effects (distortion on the lead guitar, brushes on the drums, etc.)

➢ The basis for any passages in which a soloist is expected to improvise (chord pattern, scale, melodic phrase, etc.).

Providing an annotation rather than a fully-notated score for the drums in jazz and pop idioms can save a lot of tedious work – indeed, it can be more stylistic to allow the drummer a degree of freedom – but do think carefully about showing in your annotation the kinds of patterns that you intend, where any big drum breaks or fills occur, and any passages where the drums are not required (always a good idea as it draws attention to the drummer's next contribution).

For advice on preparing a score, see page 128.

The review

When you have completed your composition you have to write a review of your work, evaluating the success of the arrangement you are going to submit. The review may be completed outside the period of 'controlled time'.

Unit 6: A Musical Performance

For this unit you have to offer performances of two or more contrasting pieces in a programme lasting 10–15 minutes. These performances can be:

➤ Solo acoustic performances

➤ Technology-based performances

➤ One solo acoustic performance and one technology-based performance.

Note that if you opt to do one of each type of performance, each must be at least 5 minutes in duration.

Live performing

A solo performance should either be:

➤ A single instrument or voice without accompaniment

➤ A single part that is accompanied by piano, guitar or backing track.

Singers especially should note that if they perform with accompaniment, it should not double their own solo line.

There needs to be accuracy in your performance, a sense of communication with your audience, and sufficient expressive qualities in the performance to show empathy for the musical character and style of the piece.

These factors should be borne in mind when you choose the music you are going to perform for the A2 exam. Your teacher(s) will no doubt be able to use their experience to give you advice. You may also want to consider the difficulty of the music. There are six marks available for the level of demand of the music you choose, with the full six being awarded to music that is consistently of a standard higher than Grade 7. However, you should exercise considerable care here: it would be much better to forego one or two marks for level of difficulty, than to choose a piece that you find very challenging. If accuracy is compromised as a result, and the pressure of trying to get round the notes impinges on your ability to interpret and communicate the music, you will lose many more than one or two marks. An easier piece may well be the better and wiser choice.

Some people have more instinct for performing 'under the spotlight' than others, but everyone benefits from gaining experience of performing. It is unadvisable, therefore, to let your A2 performance be the first formal performance of your chosen piece(s). Although some nerves can help a musician concentrate and be more dynamic in performance, the confidence that comes from knowing you have performed the piece several times before is very valuable. If previous performances have gone well, you will enjoy giving another performance, and this will come across clearly to your audience (and earn you those valuable 'communication' marks).

Look out, therefore, for every opportunity to try out your A2 pieces in other concerts. Also ask your family or friends to listen to you playing the pieces: they can be very helpful in giving you encouragement and some friendly criticism over how your performance might be improved. If your performance requires the help of an accompanist, make sure you have practised well together before any performance, and enjoy the partnership that you will have in performing your pieces.

Finally, mastery of any instrument is a long and patient process, but a hugely worthwhile and satisfying one. At the start of your A2 course you know that 30% of the marks will be awarded to your performing skills; do make sure that you have a regular routine of practice. This is certainly an area not to leave to the last moment.

Technology-based performances

There are two categories of technology-based performances that can be submitted for this unit:

➢ Sequencing

➢ Multi-track/close microphone recording.

Sequencing

The requirements for this option are as follows:

➢ The piece must be at least 48 bars long

➢ There must be six independent instrumental or vocal parts

➢ Any style is acceptable

➢ In a classical-style submission the music should involve a solo part

➢ In a pop or jazz-style submission the music should involve a vocal part.

Your work will need to show the examiner that you can control pitch and rhythm accurately; that you have a good understanding of controlling the timbre, balance and panning aspects of each instrumental or vocal part; that you have shown good attention to the expressive detail of the music; and that a clear awareness of musical style emerges from your work.

Multi-track/close microphone project

The requirements for this option are as follows:

➢ The piece must be at least 48 bars long

➢ There must be six parts, which must include independent vocal and instrumental lines

> You should use both time-based and dynamic effects (e.g. reverb, delay, etc.)

> In the final mix there should be evidence of panning/stereo.

Your work will need to show the examiner that you have achieved a good balance between parts; that you have catered for a wide dynamic range; that you have utilised panning techniques to separate sounds of similar frequencies; and that there is good quality recording across a wide range of frequencies.

Tips for both technology options

These two technology-based options will need some careful planning. Ensuring that you have access to the technology you need, when you need it, will be very important. Remember that you will only have 20 hours to complete the tasks, so you do not want to be spending any of that time getting the equipment to work. Also, remember that any musicians you require for your recording project will need time to learn their parts and rehearse together, so organisation skills will be important.

You will also need to have developed a good level of skill for using the equipment. Some people have a flair for using technology, but nothing beats being properly acquainted with the full capability of the kit you use. Working at a few practice projects in advance of the real A2 task will be very valuable, and minimise the amount of time that you will need to be consulting the instruction manual. Above all, make sure you know absolutely what to do when you want to save your work.

Glossary

A capella. Unaccompanied vocal music.

Anacrusis. One or more weak-beat notes before the first strong beat of a phrase.

Anticipation. A note played immediately before the chord to which it belongs, so creating a dissonance with the current chord.

Antiphony. Performance by different singers/instrumentalists in alternation. Often – but not always – the different groups perform similar material.

Appogiatura. An ornamental note that falls on the beat as a dissonance and then resolves by step onto the main note.

Articulation. The manner in which a series of notes are played with regards to their separation or connection – for example, staccato (separated) or legato (connected).

Atonal. Western art music that wholly or largely does not use keys or modes.

Augmentation. The lengthening of rhythmic values of a previously heard melody.

Cadence. A pair of chords signifying the end of a phrase in tonal music. See also **imperfect cadence, interrupted cadence, perfect cadence** and **plagal cadence**.

Cadenza. A showy passage for a soloist, usually without accompaniment, most commonly found towards the end of the first movement of a concerto.

Canon. A strict form of imitation, often lasting for a substantial passage or entire piece, where the second part is an exact (or almost exact) copy of the first, even if at a different pitch.

Chorale. A German hymn of the kind sung in the Lutheran (Protestant) church in the time of J. S. Bach.

Circle of 5ths. A harmonic progression in which the roots of the chords move by descending 5ths (and/or ascending 4ths), e.g. B–E–A–D–G–C, etc.

Coda. A passage (usually relatively short) concluding a piece of music.

Codetta. A passage concluding one section of a piece of music.

Col legno. A string technique of playing with the wood of the bow.

Conjunct. A conjunct melody moves by step (i.e. in major or minor seconds) rather than by larger intervals. Opposite of **disjunct**.

Countermelody. An independent melody that complements a more prominent theme.

Counterpoint. The simultaneous combination of two or more melodies that usually have different rhythms.

Cross rhythm. The use of two or more very different rhythms simultaneously in different parts. One rhythm may imply one metre (or time signature), while another implies a different one.

Development. The central section of a sonata-form movement, which elaborates on the material stated in the **exposition**.

Diatonic. Using notes that belong to the current key. A diatonic note is one that belongs to the scale of the key currently in use. For example, in D major the notes D, E and F♯ are diatonic.

Diminished 7th. A dissonant four-note chord made up of superimposed minor 3rds (for example C♯–E–G–B♭).

Diminution. The shortening of rhythmic values of a previously heard melody.

Disjunct. A disjunct melody moves by intervals larger than a 2nd. Opposite of **conjunct**.

Dissonance. Two or more sounds that give the effect of a clash. Any note not a major or minor 3rd or 6th, perfect 5th, unison or perfect octave above the lowest part sounding is strictly a dissonance.

Dominant. The fifth degree of a major or minor scale.

Dominant 7th. A four-note chord built on the dominant (fifth) note of the scale. It includes the dominant triad plus a minor 7th above the root.

Enharmonic equivalent. The same pitch notated in two different ways, e.g. B♭ and A♯.

Exposition. The first section of a sonata-form movement, which establishes the key and states the musical material to be developed later in the movement.

Fugue. A type of piece in which a theme called a 'subject' is treated in imitation by all the parts (usually with short passages called 'episodes' from which it is absent, for relief and contrast).

Glissando. A slide between two notes.

Harmonics. A technique of lightly touching a string on a string instrument to produce an artificial high sound (sometimes rather flute-like in sound).

Harmonic rhythm. The rate at which the harmony changes in a piece.

Hemiola. The articulation of two units of triple time (strong-weak-weak, strong-weak-weak) as three units of duple time (strong-weak, strong-weak, strong-weak).

Homophonic. A texture in which one part has a melody and the other parts accompany. In contrast to a **polyphonic** texture, in which each part has independent melodic interest.

Imperfect cadence. An open-ended or inconclusive cadence ending with the dominant chord (V). The preceding chord is usually I, ii or IV.

Interrupted cadence. A cadence intended to create surprise or suspense, usually consisting of chord V followed by chord VI.

Leading note. The seventh degree of a major or minor scale.

Leger lines. Additional lines used above or beneath the stave to represent notes that fall outside of its range.

Libretto. The script or words for a dramatic work that is set to music (e.g. an opera, musical or **oratorio**).

Mediant. The third degree of a major or minor scale.

Melisma. In vocal music, a single syllable sung to several notes.

Modal. Music that uses the notes of one of the Western modes (see page 15 for examples).

Modulation. The process of changing key within a single work or movement or a work.

Monophonic. A texture that consists of a single melodic line.

Motif. A short but distinctive musical idea that is developed in various ways in order to create a longer passage of music.

Oratorio. A concert piece for choir, soloists and orchestra.

Ostinato. A repeating melodic, harmonic or rhythmic **motif**, heard continuously throughout part or the whole of a piece.

Passing note. A non-harmony note approached and quitted by step in the same direction, often filling in a melodic gap of a 3rd (e.g. A between G and B, where both G and B are harmony notes).

Pedal note. A note, usually but not always appearing in the bass, that is held or repeated while the surrounding harmony changes.

Perfect cadence. Chord V or V⁷ followed by chord I at the end of a phrase – appropriate where some degree of finality is required.

Periodic phrasing. Balanced phrases of regular lengths (usually two, four or eight bars).

Pizzicato. A direction to pluck, instead of bow, string(s) on a violin, viola, cello or double bass.

Plagal cadence. Chord IV followed by chord I at the end of a phrase.

Polyphonic. A texture consisting of two or more equally important melodic lines heard together. In contrast to a **homophonic** texture, in which one part has the melody and the other parts accompany.

Recapitulation. The final section of a sonata-form movement, which restates material from the **exposition** in the tonic key.

Recitative. A movement for solo voice in an opera, cantata or **oratorio** (often before an aria) in which clear projection of words is the main concern. In many recitatives the music is functional rather than of great interest in itself, with the accompaniment often just for continuo.

Register. A specific part of the range of a voice or instrument.

Relative major and minor. Keys that have the same key signature but a different scale (e.g. F major and D minor, both with a key signature of one flat). A relative minor is three semitones lower than its relative major.

Scherzo. A fast piece usually in triple time. Often the third movement in a traditional symphony.

Sequence. The immediate repetition of a melodic or harmonic idea at a different pitch, or a succession of different pitches.

Serialism. A system of composing **atonal** music using a pre-determined series of the 12 chromatic notes to guarantee equality of all pitches.

Sonata form. Typical first-movement form of the Classical and Romantic periods. In three sections – exposition, development, recapitulation – often based on two groups of melodic material in two contrasting keys (first subject, second subject).

Subdominant. The fourth degree of a major or minor scale.

Submediant. The sixth degree of a major or minor scale.

Suspension. A suspension occurs at a change of chord, when one part hangs on to (or repeats) a note from the old chord, creating a dissonance, after which the delayed part resolves by step (usually down) to a note of the new chord.

Syncopation. Placing accents in parts of the bar that are not normally emphasised, such as on weak beats or between beats, rather than in the expected place on strong beats.

Tierce de Picardie. A major 3rd in the final tonic chord of a passage in a minor key.

Transposition. The process of writing or performing music at a higher or lower pitch than the original.

Tremolo. A rapid and continuous repetition of a single note or two alternating notes.

Trill. An ornament in which two adjacent notes rapidly and repeatedly alternate (the note bearing the trill sign and the one above it).

Tritone. An interval that is equivalent to three tones (an augmented 4th or diminished 5th).

Tutti. Italian for 'all' – a term that refers to the full ensemble, or a passage of music intended for the full ensemble.

Unison. Simultaneous performance of the same note or melody by two or more players or singers.

Vibrato. Small but fast fluctuations in the pitch of a note to add warmth and expression.

Whole-tone scale. A scale in which the interval between every successive note is a whole tone.